Business Potential of Interest free Banking

Attaur Rahman Azami

Business Potential of Interest free Banking

First Edition February 2024

Written by Attaur Rahman Azami

LIST OF CONTENTS

Content   **Page No.**

List of Tables

List of Abbreviations

CHAPTER 1: INTRODUCTION   **1-27**

1.1 Overview   1

1.2 Historical Perspectives of Interest Free Banking   2

1.3 Conventional and Interest Free Banking   2

1.4 Concept of Interest Free Banking   3

1.5 *Shariah*-Based Rule   3

    1.5.1 Prohibition of Fixed Interest Rates (*Riba*)   4

    1.5.2 Prohibition of *Gharar*   4

    1.5.3 Prohibition of Predetermined Payments   5

    1.5.4 Making Money Out of Money   5

1.6 Six Key Principles of Interest Free Banking   5

1.7 Element of Social Responsibility in Interest Free Banking   6

1.8 Contracts for Islamic Financing 6

    1.8.1 *Musharakah* 6

    1.8.2 *Mudarabah* 7

    1.8.3 *Murabahah* 7

    1.8.4 *Bai al Salam* 8

    1.8.5 *Istisna'a* 8

    1.8.6 *Ijara* 8

    1.8.7 *Qard al Hasan* 8

1.9 Structure of Islamic Financial System 9

    1.9.1 *Murabahah* 9

    1.9.2 *Ijara wa Iqtina* 9

    1.9.3 Diminishing *Musharakah* 10

    1.9.4 *Istisna'a* Contract 10

1.10 Modes of Islamic Financing 11

1.11 Sources of Funds for Islamic Banks 11

    1.11.1 Current Accounts 11

    1.11.2 Saving Deposits 12

    1.11.3 Investment Deposits 12

1.12 Gulf Investment 13

1.13 Islamic Banks 13

1.14 Islamic Banking in India Compared to Conventional Banking 13

1.15 Certain Provisions which Prohibited Interest Free Banking 14

1.16 Interest Free Banking in India   14

1.17 Issues with Islamic/Interest Free Banking in India   18

1.18 Statement of the Problem   19

1.19 Significance and Justification of the Research   21

1.20 Research Questions   21

1.21 Objectives and Hypotheses   22

1.22 Definition of Terms   25

1.23 Book Framework   26

CHAPTER 2: LITERATURE REVIEW   **28-45**

2.1 Concept of Interest Free Banking   28

2.2 Interest Free Banking: Underlying Principles   28

2.3 Different Interest Free Banking Products   29

2.4 Consumer Perspective of Interest Free Banking   30

2.5 Differences between Interest Free and Conventional Banking   31

2.6 Determinants of Bank Selection   33

2.7 *Shariah* Governance   34

2.8 Impact of Islamic Finance   35

2.9 Potential of Interest Free Banking   36

2.10 Challenges in the Growth of Interest Free Banking   37

2.11 Shortcomings of Islamic Financial Institutions   37

2.12 SWOT Analysis of Interest Free Banking   39

2.13 International Studies: Islamic Finance   40

2.14 Research Gap 43

CHAPTER 3: RESEARCH METHODOLOGY **46-72**

3.1. Research Design and Methodology 46

3.2 Research Design 46

3.3 Data Sources: Primary & Secondary Data 48

3.4 Constructs under the Study 48

3.5 Scale Development 48

3.6 Questionnaire Development and Administration 50

3.7 Pilot Study 51

3.8 Sampling Technique, Sample Size and Data Collection 52

    3.8.1 Process of Developing Scale: Administration & Scoring 52

3.9 Data Collection 53

3.10 Reliability Analysis 57

    3.10.1 Reliability Analysis: General Public 57

    3.10.2 Reliability Analysis: Bank Officials 58

3.11 Descriptive Statistics 58

    3.11.1 Descriptive Statistics: General Public's Data 58

    3.11.2 Descriptive Statistics: Bank Officials' Data 61

3.12 Normalcy Analysis of the Data 64

    3.12.1 Normalcy Analysis: General Public's Data 65

    3.12.2 Normalcy Analysis: Bank Officials' Data 67

3.13 Statistical Tools Used 70

3.14 Ethical Issues 72

CHAPTER 4: DATA ANALYSIS AND INTERPRETATION **73-141**

4.1 Introduction 73

4.2 Demographic Profile of the Respondents 73

    4.2.1 Demographic Profile of General Public 74

    4.2.2 Demographic Profile of Bank Officials 77

4.3 Research Objective 1: To test the Awareness Level of Respondents regarding IFB. 81

    4.3.1 Factor Analysis: Identifying the most important factors of Awareness of IFB for General Public. 81

    4.3.2 Factor Analysis: Identifying the most important factors of Awareness of IFB for Bank Officials. 85

    4.3.3 Chi Square Analysis: Difference between Male and Female Respondents among General Public regarding Awareness Level of IFB. 88

    4.3.4 Chi Square Analysis: Difference between Government Bank and Private Bank Respondents among Bank Officials regarding Awareness Level of IFB. 89

4.4 Research Objective 2: To identify whether current Banks (Private as well as Govt.) will be ready to introduce IFB or not if investors are ready to adopt it. 89

    4.4.1 Factor Analysis: Identifying the most important factors of Acceptability about IFB for General Public. 89

    4.4.2 Factor Analysis: Identifying the most important factors of Acceptability about IFB for Bank Officials. 92

    4.4.3 Regression Analysis: Impact of Awareness Level on Acceptability Level from the perspective of General Public. 94

    4.4.4 Regression Analysis: Impact of Awareness Level on Acceptability Level from the perspective of Bank Officials. 95

4.4.5 Chi-Square Analysis: Difference between Male and Female Respondents among General Public regarding Acceptability of IFB.   96

4.4.6 Chi-Square Analysis: Difference between Government Bank and Private Bank Respondents among Bank Officials regarding Acceptability Level of IFB.   97

4.5 Research Objective 3: To explore the Business Potential of IFB in India.   98

4.5.1 Factor Analysis: Identifying the most important factors of Business Potential of IFB and Religious aspects for General Public.   98

4.5.2 Factor Analysis: Identifying the most important factors of Business potential of IFB for Bank Officials.   100

4.6 Research Objective 4: To Identify the Impact of Religion on Investing Behavior of Respondents.   108

4.7 Research Objective 5: To identify the influence of demographic variables (Age, Gender, Educational Qualifications, Occupation, Monthly Income) on Investing Behavior of Respondents.   116

4.7.1 Chi Square Analysis: Difference between Respondents' Investing Behavior and their Age.   117

4.7.2 Chi Square Analysis: Difference between Respondents' Investing Behavior and their Genders.   122

4.7.3 Chi Square Analysis: Difference between Respondents' Investing Behavior and their Educational Qualifications.   124

4.7.4 Chi Square Analysis: Difference between Respondents' Investing Behavior and their Occupation.   127

4.7.5 Chi Square Analysis: Difference between Respondents' Investing Behavior and their Monthly Income.   134

CHAPTER 5: FINDINGS, CONCLUSION & RECOMMENDATIONS   142-157

5.1 Findings of the Study   142

5.1.1 Hypotheses wise Findings   143

    5.2 Discussion and Conclusion   146

5.3 Suggestions   153

5.4 Limitations   155

5.5 Future Scope   156

BIBLIOGRAPHY   **158-167**

LIST OF TABLES

Table 3.1- Variables   50

Table 3.2- Sample Size   54

Table 3.3- Distribution of respondents: city wise- In case of General Public   54

Table 3.4- Distribution of respondents: city wise- In case of Bank Officials   54

Table 3.5- Statistics: General Public   55

Table 3.6- Statistics: Bank Officials   56

Table 3.7- Reliability Statistics General Public   57

Table 3.8- Reliability Statistics Bank Officials   58

Table 3.9- Descriptive Statistics: General Public   58

Table 3.10- Descriptive Statistics: Bank Officials   61

Table 3.11- Tests of Normality: General Public   65

Table 3.12- Tests of Normality: Bank Officials   67

Table 4.1- City (General Public)   74

Table 4.2- Age   74

Table 4.3- Gender   74

Table 4.4- Religion   75

Table 4.5- Marital Status   75

Table 4.6- Educational Qualifications   75

Table 4.7- Occupation   76

Table 4.8- Monthly Income   76

Table 4.9- Major Banking Services Availed   76

Table 4.10- Major Purpose of Availing Banking Services 77

Table 4.11- Investment Preference 77

Table 4.12- City (Bank Officials) 77

Table 4.13- Age 78

Table 4.14- Gender 78

Table 4.15- Religion 78

Table 4.16- Marital Status 79

Table 4.17- Educational Qualifications 79

Table 4.18- Designation 79

Table 4.19- Type of Bank 80

Table 4.20- Distribution of Private and Government Banks City wise 80

Table 4.21- Factor Analysis of Awareness (General Public) 81

Table 4.22- Total Variance Explained 82

Table 4.23- Rotated Component Matrix 83

Table 4.24- Factor Analysis of Awareness (Bank Officials) 85

Table 4.25- Total Variance Explained 85

Table 4.26- Rotated Component Matrix 86

Table 4.27- Chi Square Tests: Gender wise Awareness Level (General Public) 88

Table 4.28- Gender wise Awareness Level Cross Tabulation 88

Table 4.29- Chi Square Tests: Bank wise Awareness Level 89

Table 4.30- Factor Analysis of Acceptability (General Public) 89

Table 4.31- Total Variance Explained 90

Table 4.32- Rotated Component Matrix   90

Table 4.33- Factor Analysis of Acceptability (Bank Officials)   92

Table 4.34-Total Variance Explained   92

Table 4.35- Rotated Component Matrix   93

Table 4.36- ANOVA: Impact of Awareness on Acceptability (General
Public)   94

Table 4.37- ANOVA: Impact of Awareness on Acceptability (Bank
Officials)   95

Table 4.38- Model Summary   95

Table 4.39- Coefficient   96

Table 4.40- Chi Square Tests: Gender wise Acceptability Level (General
Public)   96

Table 4.41- Acceptability Level Cross Tabulation   97

Table 4.42- Chi Square Tests: Bank wise Acceptability Level   97

Table 4.43- Factor Analysis of Business Potential (General Public)   98

Table 4.44- Total Variance Explained   98

Table 4.45- Rotated Component Matrix   99

Table 4.46- Factor Analysis of Business Potential (Bank Officials)   101

Table 4.47- Total Variance Explained   101

Table 4.48- Rotated Component Matrix   102

Table 4.49- ANOVA: Impact of Awareness Level on Business Potential
(General Public)   103

Table 4.50- Model Summary   103

Table 4.51- Coefficient   104

Table 4.52- ANOVA: Impact of Awareness Level on Business Potential (Bank Officials)   104

Table 4.53- ANOVA: Impact of Acceptability Level on Business Potential (General Public)   105

Table 4.54- Model Summary   105

Table 4.55- Coefficient   105

Table 4.56- ANOVA: Impact of Acceptability Level on Business Potential (Bank Officials)   106

Table 4.57- Model Summary   106

Table 4.58- Coefficient   107

Table 4.59- Chi Square Tests: Gender wise Business Potential (General Public)   107

Table 4.60- Chi Square Tests: Gender wise Business Potential (Bank Officials)   108

Table 4.61- Chi-Square Tests: Difference between Religion and Investing Behavior (Emphasizes on social activities)   108

Table 4.62- Crosstab: Emphasizes social activities   108

Table 4.63- Chi-Square Tests: Difference between Religion and Investing Behavior (Prohibition of excessive risk/uncertainty)   109

Table 4.64- Crosstab: That works on the principle of Prohibition of excessive risk/uncertainty   109

Table 4.65- Chi-Square Tests: Difference between Religion and Investing Behavior (Transactions that are backed by a tangible asset)   110

Table 4.66- Crosstab: Only allows the transactions that are backed by a tangible asset   111

Table 4.67- Chi-Square Tests: Difference between Religion and Investing Behavior (Does not approve financing of alcohol)   112

Table 4.68- Crosstab: Does not approve financing of alcohol 112

Table 4.69- Chi-Square Tests: Difference between Religion and Investing Behavior (Does not approve financing of pork) 113

Table 4.70- Crosstab: Does not approve financing of pork 114

Table 4.71- Chi-Square Tests: Difference between Religion and Investing Behavior (Does not approve financing of ammunitions) 115

Table 4.72- Crosstab: Does not approve financing of ammunitions 115

Table 4.73- Chi Square Tests: Difference between Investing Behavior and Age (Tobacco/Alcohol Products) 117

Table 4.74- Crosstab: Tobacco/Alcohol Products 117

Table 4.75- Chi Square Tests: Difference between Investing Behavior and Age (All Non-Vegetarian Products) 118

Table 4.76- Crosstab: All Non-Vegetarian Products 118

Table 4.77- Chi Square Tests: Difference between Investing Behavior and Age (Arms and Ammunition) 119

Table 4.78- Chi Square Tests: Difference between Investing Behavior and Age (Non-Environment Friendly Products) 120

Table 4.79- Crosstab: Non-Environment Friendly Products 120

Table 4.80- Chi Square Tests: Difference between Investing Behavior and Age (Products that involves animal cruelty) 121

Table 4.81- Crosstab: Products that involves animal cruelty 121

Table 4.82- Chi Square Tests: Difference between Investing Behavior and Gender (Tobacco/Alcohol products) 122

Table 4.83- Chi Square Tests: Difference between Investing Behavior and Gender (All non-vegetarian Products) 122

Table 4.84- Chi Square Tests: Difference between Investing Behavior and Gender (Arms and Ammunition)   123

Table 4.85- Chi Square Tests: Difference between Investing Behavior and Gender (Non-Environment Friendly Products)   123

Table 4.86- Chi Square Tests: Difference between Investing Behavior and Gender (Products that involves Animal Cruelty)   124

Table 4.87- Chi Square Tests: Difference between Investing Behavior and Educational Qualifications (Tobacco/Alcohol Products)   124

Table 4.88- Crosstab: Tobacco/Alcohol Products   124

Table 4.89- Chi Square Test: Difference between Investing Behavior and Educational Qualifications (All non-vegetarian Products)   126

Table 4.90- Chi Square Tests: Difference between Investing Behavior and Educational Qualifications (Arms and Ammunition)   126

Table 4.91- Chi Square Tests: Difference between Investing Behavior and Educational Qualifications (Non-Environment Friendly Products)   126

Table 4.92- Chi Square Tests: Difference between Investing Behavior and Educational Qualifications (Products that involves animal cruelty)   127

Table 4.93- Chi Square Tests: Difference between Investing Behavior and Occupation (Tobacco/Alcohol Products)   127

Table 4.94- Crosstab: Tobacco/Alcohol Products   128

Table 4.95- Chi Square Tests: Difference between Investing Behavior and Occupation (All non-vegetarian Products)   129

Table 4.96- Crosstab: All non-vegetarian Products   129

Table 4.97- Chi Square Tests: Difference between Investing Behavior and Occupation (Arms and Ammunition)   130

Table 4.98- Crosstab: Arms and Ammunition   130

Table 4.99- Chi Square Tests: Difference between Investing Behavior and Occupation (Non-Environment Friendly Products) 131

Table 4.100- Crosstab: Non-Environment Friendly Products 132

Table 4.101- Chi Square Tests: Difference between Investing Behavior and Occupation (Products that involves animal cruelty) 133

Table 4.102- Crosstab: Products that involves Animal Cruelty 133

Table 4.103- Chi Square Tests: Difference between Investing Behavior and Monthly Income (Tobacco/Alcohol Products) 134

Table 4.104- Crosstab: Tobacco/Alcohol Products 134

Table 4.105- Chi Square Tests: Difference between Investing Behavior and Monthly Income (All non-vegetarian Products) 135

Table 4.106- Crosstab: All Non-Vegetarian Products 136

Table 4.107- Chi Square Tests: Difference between Investing Behavior and Monthly Income (Arms and Ammunition) 137

Table 4.108- Crosstab: Arms and Ammunition 137

Table 4.109- Chi Square Tests: Difference between Investing Behavior and Monthly Income (Non-Environment Friendly Products) 138

Table 4.110- Crosstab: Non-Environment Friendly Products 139

Table 4.111- Chi Square Tests: Difference between Investing Behavior and Monthly Income (Products that involves animal cruelty) 140

Table 4.112- Crosstab: Products that involves Animal Cruelty 140

LIST OF ABBREVIATIONS

IFB	-	Interest Free Banking
IFBS	-	Interest Free Banking System
IB	-	Islamic Banks
IBS	-	Islamic Banking System
IFIs	-	Islamic Financial Institutions
SSB	-	*Shariah* Supervisory Board
NPLS	-	Non-Profit and Loss Sharing
PLS	-	Profit-and-Loss Sharing
PSIA	-	Profit Sharing Investment Account
CFSR	-	Committee on Financial Sector Reform
CAGR	-	Compound Annual Growth Rate
CIBAFI	-	General Council of Islamic Banks and Financial Institutions
TDS	-	Tax Deduction at Source
RBI	-	Reserve Bank of India

CHAPTER 1: INTRODUCTION

1.1 Overview

Interest Free Banking is based on the Islamic **Shariah's** *"Fiqhul-Muamalaat"* doctrine. There are two main tenets: the first is that parties should split profits and losses; the second prohibits lenders and investors from engaging in the collection and payment of interest. The *"Riba"* of interest collection is expressly forbidden under **Shariah**. Additionally, "investments in pork, gambling, entertainment, and other banned goods are severely prohibited. In 51 nations, including the United States and the United Kingdom, there were more than 500 Islamic Banks" (Ansari A. & Tariq H., 2016).

Thus, **IFB** was developed to meet customer demand for banking services that complied with **Shariah** regulations. Islamic thought views "Interest Free Bank as a **Halaal** alternative that would protect the interests of the servants from harms associated with **Haraam** that is prohibited by the Almighty saying (God has permitted the sale and prohibited usury)" **Al-Baqarah**: 2:75. The fundamental justification for the ban on interest is that it is oppressive and unfair. Rich people who can lend can also charge interest on those loans, allowing them to amass wealth at the expense of those who are in need of it (Ansari A. & Tariq H., 2016).

The Islamic Financial System was reportedly standing on solid ground, particularly in the aftermath of the 2008 financial crisis due to the presence of financial institutions in numerous nations. Currently, the UAE, Saudi Arabia, Bahrain, Britain, Malaysia, and Singapore are vying with one another to establish themselves as the world's leading centres for **IFB**. The Islamic finance sector has now begun to grow outside of the major Muslim nations, transcending national boundaries and religious restrictions. This industry has experienced tremendous expansion in Europe, the "United Kingdom", "Australia", "Hong Kong", "Korea", and the "United States" (Ansari A & Tariq H, 2016).

"A nominal zero interest rate, according to Friedman (1969), is a requirement for the best distribution of resources. By examining general equilibrium models, it was discovered that zero interest rates are both necessary and sufficient for allocative efficiency" (Cole & Kocherlakota, 1998).

Additionally, studies have shown that "interest free (profit-and-loss sharing) systems are more practical and effective than interest-based systems" (Chapra 1985; Mirakhor, 1997).

1

Based on the strong performance displayed by Islamic housing mortgages during the recent financial crisis, Basainey Ebrahima Jammeh (2010) found that "despite the ongoing decline in consumer confidence in U.S. financial institutions during the post-crisis period, the future of Islamic financial intermediation in the U.S. appears to be promising". This is the main factor behind the rise in popularity of **IFB**. Following the above discussion, the current study's goal is to examine the business potential of **IFB** in India, specifically with regard to the state of Uttar Pradesh.

1.2 Historical Perspectives of Interest Free Banking

IFB is not an entirely new idea. "The decolonization of Middle Eastern nations had a significant impact on the development of **IFB**" (Birben B, 2013).

- Mit Ghamr established an Egyptian saving bank based on profit sharing in 1963. It was effectively **IFB** based on the principles of rural cooperative banking.
- In response to the 1973 oil crisis, an Islamic Financial Development Bank was established. The Islamic Development Bank, the first contemporary Islamic Bank founded on *Shariah* principles, was created in 1975 as an intergovernmental bank.
- The first Islamic Bank was founded in Malaysia in 1983, but it was not permitted to do regular banking.
- **IFB**was accepted by traditional banking in 1993.
- The British Islamic Bank was established in 2004 and was the first non-Muslim nation to do so.

1.3 Conventional and Interest Free Banking

"Currently, Interest Free Banks function in two ways: first, as full-fledged Islamic Banks that are governed by Islamic law and use *Shariah*-compliant financial instruments; and second, as Islamic Banking Windows. These specialised windows run within traditional banks and serve clients who want to use financial services and products that comply with *Shariah*". 'The Banking Regulation Act', 'The 1949 Negotiable Instruments Act', 'The Reserve Bank of India Act 1938', and 'The Cooperative Society Act' all govern banks in India. "Although **IFB** is not specifically prohibited by Indian banking rules, there are numerous provisions that make it practically impossible" (Ahangar G. B. & Ganie A. H., 2013).

2

1.4 Concept of Interest Free Banking

The demand for **IFB** is on the rise, leading to the successful operation of these banks in the "Middle East" and beyond. The fundamental principle of **IFB** involves not only profit-sharing but also risk-sharing. This concept is gaining widespread acceptance in the "Middle East" and other predominantly Muslim nations. Residents in these regions are undergoing a shift in their investment perspectives, aligning their financial activities with the principles of Islamic faith. As a result, there is a growing inclination among Muslims to explore investment avenues that adhere to Islamic principles.

"**IFB** or Islamic investment concepts are based on the Islamic economic system, which includes things like not taking interest on deposits and paying an obligatory tax (*Zakat* System) of 2.5% on the total. As a result of these Western banks' exploration of the nature of **IFB** and its operations over the past few years, these Western banks have started Islamic investment units in their banks (Khan, M. A., 1994)".

1.5 *Shariah*-Based Rule

According to recent reports by the 'General Council of Islamic Banks' and 'Financial Institutions (CIBAFI)' and the 'World Bank' (2017), "*Shariah* governance is considered a crucial requirement for Islamic Financial Institutions (IFIs), particularly Islamic Banks (IBs)". The report emphasizes the pivotal role played by the *Shariah* Supervisory Board (SSB) in overseeing IFIs, ensuring their adherence to Islamic jurisprudence and principles (*Shariah*).

"The differences in the *Shariah* governance practises of IBs, particularly between countries with specific and comprehensive *Shariah* governance legislation and those that do not, may come into question in the absence of a global *Shariah* governance framework. Further questions may also reveal which functions or elements, other than the *Shariah* Supervisory Board (SSB), are involved in the implementation of *Shariah* governance in IBs" (Ghannadian & Goswami, 2004).

- **Things that Islamic Finance Forbids**

The following section discusses the fundamental tenets of the Islamic economic order, which serves as the framework for **IFB**.

1.5.1 Prohibition of Fixed Interest Rates (*Riba*)

"The outlawing of *Riba* is seen as one of the most essential and a noble task in Islamic Law and it also has significant practical implications that set Islamic money apart from conventional non-Muslim banking. Islamic finance, which is founded on the *Shariah*, has a fundamentally different risk-reward philosophy than traditional, interest-based finance" (Ghannadian & Goswami, 2004).

"Rewards without commensurate risk and preferential rewards are not permitted; *Riba* (commonly referred to as interest) is impermissible under the *Shariah* as it is both a reward without commensurate risk and a preferential reward to one party (whether a debt provider or an equity provider). Trading and partnership or joint venture arrangements are more appropriate risk-reward paradigms" (Ghannadian & Goswami, 2004).

"Money is not an asset that can earn money; it is a measured store of value and a medium of exchange. Every financial transaction must involve a tangible asset, with some exceptions, such as intellectual property. Predetermined fixed returns are generally not permissible, as are guarantees or assurances of return of or on capital. Additionally, the use of money as a commodity is not acceptable under the *Shariah*" (Ghannadian & Goswami, 2004).

"What is unacceptable is not an addition obtained through earned profit; rather, the moral lapse lies in obtaining an increase free of charge, without giving value in exchange, or exerting effort - in other words, without doing a shred of work" (Ghannadian & Goswami, 2004).

- **Profit and *Riba***

Profit arises from engaging in trade, which encompasses concrete transactions involving the exchange of goods or services for currency or other commodities. This concept aligns with the teachings of the Qur'an, which states: "God has permitted trading and forbidden *Riba*" (Quran, 2:275). In this context, *Riba* pertains to the practice of lending money over a designated period and imposing a predetermined interest on the principal amount.

1.5.2 Prohibition of *Gharar*

For example, "gambling or any transaction in which the buyer pays significantly less than what the object is worth, and then either takes the object at this cheap price or loses the money; thus, the results depend on chance. Such transactions are highly risky and may have unfavourable consequences. *Gharar* is defined as trade with excessive risk emerging from unknown factors, and it deals with issues concerning contractual uncertainty arising from factors with unknown outcome" (Al-Suwailem, 2000).

1.5.3 Prohibition of Predetermined Payments

Islam permits only one type of loan, called ***Qard al Hasan***, where the lender does not charge any interest or additional amount over the money lent. According to one Islamic scholar, "traditional Muslim jurists have construed this principle so strictly that it emphasises that any associated or indirect benefit over and above the actual amount of principal is prohibited" (Kettell B., 2011).

1.5.4 Making Money Out of Money

Khan (1994) claimed that "the concept of the time value of money has rational difficulties and violates the ***Shariah*** prohibition of interest," whereas Gambling & Karim (1991) claimed that "Islam does not recognise the time value of money on the basis that time is not a production factor like labour and capital, therefore it cannot generate a yield by itself. It is unacceptable to use money to make more money".

"Money, in Islam, is only a medium of exchange, a way of defining the value of a thing, and as such, should not be allowed to generate more money, via fixed interest payments, simply by being deposited in a bank or lent to someone else. Making money from money is not acceptable according to Islamic law" (Kettell B., 2011).

1.6 Six Key Principles of Interest Free Banking

Kettell B. (2011) noted "the following Islamic principles of money that can be broken down into six distinct concepts and are found in the Quran, which Muslims believe to be the precise words of God as given to the Prophet Mohammed".

1. ***Riba***, which refers to predetermined loan repayments in the form of interest, is strictly prohibited.
2. The Islamic system is built on the principle of profit and loss sharing.
3. Making money with the intent to spend it is not allowed; all financial transactions must be secured by assets.

4. Speculative actions are not permitted.

5. Contracts must be approved by the *Shariah*.

6. Contracts have inherent value (Kettell B, 2011).

1.7 Element of Social Responsibility in Interest Free Banking

"Islamic businesses and individuals bear significant responsibilities toward the communities in which they operate. The Quran and the teachings of Prophet Muhammad (peace be upon him) underscore the social roles of every Muslim, emphasizing the importance of contributing positively to society. all Muslims are seen as brothers and should help each other communally. Islamic Banks usually undertake activities that reflect their social role in the community. Social activities are emphasised in Islamic Banks' articles of association as part of their objectives and functions" (El-Ashker, 1987).

"Islamic Banks are described as having a 'social face' (Mashhour 1996). Their social role is reflected in their provision of the *Qard al Hasan*, which helps borrowers to achieve social goals such as marriage, also in other charitable social activities".

1.8 Contracts for Islamic Financing

"The most significant Islamic financial contracts will be described in this section by underpinning the notion for each technique and can be compared to an existent Western financial instrument, which distinguishes Islamic Banks from Conventional Banks" (Usmani, 2002).

1.8.1 *Musharakah*

"The *Musharakah* mode is based on both the parties, the bank and the entrepreneur (the owner manager), agreeing to form a new partnership that may resemble a company; the capital of this partnership will be provided by the two parties. The owner manager will be entitled to receive a salary for his work, and the remaining profit will be distributed as agreed upon at the time of affecting the contract between the parties, which may not coincide with the ratio of financial risk" (Usmani, 2002). Islamic scholars agree on "the proportion of losses that should be shared in the event of a loss according to each partner's portion of the investment, the loss for each partner should be calculated" (Lewis & Algaoud, 2001).

6

Errico & Farahbaksh (1998) claimed that "the *Musharakah* contract is typically used in long-term investment projects and that it is well suited for financing private or public companies and participating in project financing for short, medium, and long-term periods".

"*Musharakah* contracts give the bank the right to participate in the management of the project and monitoring its performance. This form of financing enables the banks to get more information and enrich the experience of the management of the project with financial experiences. It is like venture capital in the conventional system which involves a higher degree of risk, and the partners may lose in addition to their profit all or part of their capital. However, partners' losses are limited to their investment in the case of insolvency and the manager's personal assets and the bank's other assets will not be called upon Since there is no market for such shares; therefore, the partners may agree to terminate. If one of the parties wants the termination of *Musharakah*, while the other partner or parties wish to continue in the business, this can be achieved by mutual agreement of the two parties, where the partner who wants to continue will buy the share of the terminated partner. *Musharakah* may take several forms of agreements; financing of a single transaction, diminishing *Musharakah*, working capital and fixed capital" (Wilson, 1997 & Usmani, 2002).

1.8.2 *Mudarabah*

"A *Mudarabah* agreement is a trust-based financing arrangement in which an investor (Islamic Bank) entrusts capital to an agent (*Mudarib*) for a project; profits are based on a prearranged and agreed-upon ratio. A *Mudarabah* agreement is similar to a western-style limited partnership, with one party contributing capital while the other runs the business; profits are distributed based on negotiated percentage of ownership" (Usmani, 2002).

1.8.3 *Murabahah*

"The most popular form of financing in **IFB** is called *Murabahah*; it was originally a sale contract where the client asked the bank to buy a certain product for him, the bank acquired the product, resold it to the client in a different contract, disclosed the cost of the product, and added-up in the form of a predetermined markup; the markup represents the bank profit and a payment for the risk involved in the financing; in a way" (Presley, J. R. 1988).

1.8.4 *Bai al Salam*

"The Islamic Bank may, through this agreement, enter into a contract with a client for the advance purchase of his products, describing the product in full, including its quality, price, and place and time of delivery, and paying the agreed sum at the time of the agreement's entry. When the product is created and supplied to the bank on the designated date, the bank has the right to sell the product" (Ba-Owaidan, 1994).

1.8.5 *Istisna'a*

"If the seller does not have the capacity to manufacture or construct the commodity, it may contract it to a third party, which is known as a parallel *Istisna'a*. *Shariah* requires that the price should be agreed upon when signing the contract, and cannot be changed for reasons such as increase. In this case, Islamic Banks are the seller" (Maali B., 2005).

1.8.6 *Ijara*

"An Islamic Bank (lessor) leases the asset to a client (lessee) for agreed-upon lease payments for a specified period of time with no option for ownership for the lessee. *Ijara* is an Islamic leasing concept that is comparable to the operating and finance leases used in the west (Zaher & Hassan, 2001)".

"Direct leasing finance, which allows the client to use the equipment without needing to own it, makes it easier to get new equipment after the hiring period is over, while a lease and purchase contract necessitates that the bank purchase the equipment on behalf of the clients and retain ownership until the end of the hire purchase period" (Lewis & Algaoud, 2001). "Despite the widespread use of leasing financing in Western institutions, there are important distinctions between Islamic leasing contracts based on *Ijara* and conventional leasing. According to *Shariah* law, the lessor is required to manage, maintain, and insure the leased assets, whereas under conventional leasing contracts, the lessee is typically in charge of these tasks" (Wilson, 1997).

1.8.7 *Qard al Hasan*

"The Islamic Banks offer such loans for welfare purposes; typically, they are given to those starting a social activity, like marriage or study, or those incurring exceptional expenses due to illness or accidents. *Qard al Hasan* is a beneficence loan; it represents a non-interest bearing loan, in fact to allow the borrower to use the loan for a period of time on the basis that the same amount of money would be repaid at the end of the period" (AAOIFI, 1999).

1.9 Structure of Islamic Financial System

The swift evolution of **IFB**, characterized by substantial expansion and advancements in the field of Islamic finance, has gained growing significance in addressing the evolving needs of the new economy. To facilitate Muslims in acquiring homes in accordance with their religious beliefs, four distinct structures have been implemented. These structures not only provide financial solutions but also adhere to the principles outlined in Islamic teachings.

Structure of Islamic Financial System

- *Murabahah*
- *Ijara* wa *Iqtina*
- Diminishing *Musharakah*
- *Istisna'a* Contract

1.9.1 *Murabahah*

Murabahah is also known as *"Bai'a Bi-thaman Ajil"*, signifying a deferred payment sale. This structure allows individuals to acquire property through a deferred payment plan, introducing a level of flexibility that adheres to Islamic principles. By incorporating the *Murabahah* mechanism into home financing, Islamic finance institutions aim to provide a *Sharia*-compliant alternative that mirrors traditional home purchase processes while upholding the ethical and legal standards outlined in Islamic teachings.

1.9.2 *Ijara wa Iqtina*

In this transactional model, the investor pledges to sell, while the customer commits to purchasing the selected property. The customer, functioning as the lessee, chooses a property, and the investor, in the role of the lessor, executes the purchase. Subsequently, an operational property lease is established between the investor (lessor) and the customer (lessee), where the customer pays rent. Simultaneously, the customer contributes to a savings fund, structured to accumulate to a level that enables the eventual purchase of the property from the investor.

"The period of the lease and the rent payments may be made such that the final payments are only symbolic. The concept requires a **Shariah** modification to the conventional house purchase process to allow the investor or the bank to take the place of the consumer in the purchase contract. It gave the option at the end to buy the item from the lessor (and owner) at a pre-specified residual value" (Omar M, 2013).

1.9.3 Diminishing *Musharakah*

Diminishing *Musharakah* represents a unique iteration of *Musharakah*, culminating in the eventual full ownership of the asset or project by the client. These principles are applicable universally to any project and materialize through the following operational dynamics:

The Islamic Bank assumes the role of a financial partner, furnishing either full or partial contributions to a project, along with a predetermined income projection. An agreement is formalized between the bank and the partner, outlining the distribution of profits between the entities. It's noteworthy that the agreement refrains from explicitly specifying the ultimate outcome of the project—specifically, the acquisition of the asset or project by the client.

According to (Omar M., 2013) the process of Diminishing *Musharakah* in the context of home financing, involves four key steps:

1. "The bank collaborates with the customer/partner to establish a specific gradual approach for divesting its share of the house. Simultaneously, the bank extends a portion of the capital required for the house purchase in its capacity as a participant.

2. In exchange for eventual complete ownership of the property, the customer or partner contributes a portion of the capital needed to build the home and agrees to pay a certain sum in rent.

3. The bank indicates its willingness to sell a particular percentage of its capital share, with the rental component reducing, in accordance with the terms of the agreement.

4. The ownership is transferred to the customer/partner when the customer/partner pays the bank the cost of that percentage of capital".

1.9.4 *Istisna'a* Contract

"With an *Istisna'a* contract, the consumer asks the bank to finance the building or a house. The bank contracts with a builder or the consumer to construct the house using the bank's cash.Following the completion of the development, there may be an outright cash sale, a *Murabahah* sale, a *Ijara wa Iqtina* sale, or a diminishing *Musharakah* partnership" (Omar M., 2013).

1.10 Modes of Islamic Financing

"Islamic modes of financing are designed in such a way that they affect both the assets and liabilities of bank's balance sheet and are divided into two major categories. They are based on PLS (profit-and-loss sharing, which is a core mode) principle and NPLS (non-profit and loss sharing, which is a marginal mode). These modes are central to formulating, designing and structuring all financial products and instruments of banking, insurance and capital markets within the Islamic financial industry. From the offset, one can observe that they are both performing tremendously different actions; this is because **IFB** is based on Islamic law, and hence all transactions, product features, business approaches, investments aims, and responsibilities are based purely on *Shariah* principles, which are completely different from conventional banking" (Mondher B., 2013).

1.11 Sources of Funds for Islamic Banks

"Under a dual window banking operation, the initial paid-up capital is typically given on *Qard al Hasan* basis (benevolent loan that is free of interest from conventional counterpart), so there should be no problem with regard to the source of the funds" (Omar M, 2013). However, the original source of Islamic funds must be determined to ensure that it come from "*Halal*" sources.

Generally speaking, Islamic Banks that operate under an **IFB** system rely on the following sources of funding:

1.11.1 Current Accounts

"Current accounts, occasionally classified as 'other accounts' in financial statements, are diligently managed by all Islamic Banks on behalf of their clients, encompassing both individuals and businesses. These accounts are designed to enhance customer convenience and ensure the secure storage of deposits. The key characteristics of these accounts include (Omar M, 2013):

- The depositor is not given a portion of the bank's earnings, interest, or other returns; rather, the bank guarantees the complete return of these deposits upon demand.
- Depositors grant the bank authorization to utilize their funds at the bank's own risk. Consequently, the bank stands to gain financially from deploying these funds and, in turn, assumes responsibility for any associated losses.
- Both deposits and withdrawals are not subject to any restrictions.
- Account holders typically have the ability to draw checks against their accounts".

1.11.2 Saving Deposits

"All Islamic Banks operate savings accounts, but there are some differences in how these accounts are run. A typical example is Malaysian Islamic Bank, which defines savings deposits. The bank accepts deposits from its customers looking for safe custody of their funds and a degree of convenience in their use along with the possibility of some profits on the principle of *Al-Wadia*" (Omar M, 2013).

1.11.3 Investment Deposits

Investment deposits, alternatively termed as profit and loss sharing (PLS) accounts, investment accounts, or participatory accounts, mirror the structure of term deposits or time deposits found in conventional banks. These accounts operate on the foundational principles of the *Mudarabah* contract.

According to (Kettel B, 2011) key characteristics of *Mudarabah* that significantly impact the sources of bank funds include:

- "The distribution of profits between the parties involved must consistently adhere to a proportional basis, eliminating the possibility of a lump sum or guaranteed return.
- The investor is shielded from losses that surpass the initially provided capital. This feature safeguards the investor's exposure, limiting potential financial drawbacks.
- Apart from investing time and effort, the *Mudarib* (entrepreneur or manager) does not bear a share of the losses incurred. This provision establishes a clear demarcation between the investor's capital and the *Mudarib's* efforts, safeguarding the *Mudarib* from absorbing financial losses beyond their own contribution.
- The *Mudarabah* may be used generally or for a particular purpose".

12

1.12 Gulf Investment

"At present, almost all the money is deposited in the Islamic Banking windows in London, New York, Zurich, and Frankfurt. However, due to fund manipulation in the recent past, they are looking for a safe investment destination. India could well be that destination with the establishment of Islamic Banks, as people from that region are investing their surplus in *Shariah*-compliant institutions" (Raqeeb A., 2010).

1.13 Islamic Banks

"Globally, there are now 47 financial institutions with more than $10 billion in *Shariah*-compliant assets, up one from the previous year. Of these institutions, 27 recorded a pre-tax profit of more than $500 million in 2019. The industry has doubled in size over the past decade and has experienced a compound annual growth rate (CAGR) of around 10.8% since 2006".

1.14 Interest Free Banking in India Compared to Conventional Banking

1. **Current Account:** In this regard, comparisons between **IFB** and traditional banking are possible. Interest is not permitted in current accounts, which are regarded as **IFB** in the Indian Banking System.

2. **Savings Accounts (*Al-Wadia*):** Savings accounts are similar to investment accounts. "Section 21 of the Banking Regulation Act of 1949" forbids **IFB**, which is a cornerstone of Islamic Banking, and mandates the payment of interest on savings accounts.

3. **Investment Accounts (*Mudarabah*):** Investment Accounts are restricted by "Section 21 of the Banking Regulation Act of 1949", preventing banks from utilizing them to invest in equity funds. Conversely, under **IFB** laws, investments are accepted for either a defined or unlimited period, with the understanding that these investments will share a specified percentage of the profit (or loss) with the bank. The capital invested is not guaranteed.

4. **Project Financing:** The cornerstone of **IFB**, profit sharing and partnership contracts, are prohibited by Sections 5 and 6 of the "Banking Regulation Act of 1949".

5. **Home Financing:** The bank acquires assets and leases them to clients for a rental fee, incorporating the cost of the home along with a profit margin. Throughout the repayment

period, the bank maintains ownership of the assets. Upon the conclusion of the final payment, ownership of the home is then transferred to the customer.

1.15 Certain Provisions which Prohibited Interest Free Banking

Certain provisions of Banking Regulation Act, 1949 (Act10 of 1949) prohibit **IFB** in India:

- The Banking Regulation Act's "Sections 5(b) and 5(c)" forbid banks from investing on a profit-loss-sharing basis.
- "Section 8 of the Banking Regulation Act of 1949" forbids dealing in the direct or indirect purchase, sale, or barter of products.
- "Section 9 of the Banking Regulation Act of 1949" forbids banks from using any type of real estate for purposes other than their own private use.
- "Section 21 of Banking Regulation Act of 1949" requires the payment of interest.

1.16 Interest Free Banking in India

Former RBI Governor D. Subbarao has proposed the introduction of **IFB** in India, urging the government to amend existing laws to accommodate such a system. In the pursuit of promoting inclusive economic growth, the distinguished High-Level Committee on Financial Sector Reform (CFSR) within the Planning Commission of India in 2008, chaired by Dr. Raghuram Rajan, advocated for the integration of Interest-Free Finance and Banking as an integral component of mainstream banking. Despite the current practice of **IFB** in India through Non-Banking Financial Companies (NBFCs) and *Baitul Mal* (Islamic Treasury), its operational scale remains relatively modest. These organizations primarily operate at a local level, catering to specific markets.

Numerous Indian institutions, some of which are owned by the government, have expressed interest in this expanding market segment. For example, the Kerala government-owned KSIDC introduced "Al-Barakah Financial Services Ltd". The "GIC of India administers an Islamic insurance program and some mutual fund schemes specifically adhere to Islamic law in their investment practices. The first of its type in India is the TASIS index on the Bombay Stock Exchange, which only includes *Shariah*-compliant stocks. "Usefulness of **IFB** in India despite its roots in religious precepts lies in the Islamic finance, which is also a viable investment strategy based on risk sharing" (Khadar A. & Aneesh A, 2019). "It makes financial sense for the countries that have embraced Islamic financing. Islamic finance focuses on promoting and facilitating investments in legitimate economic activity and societal welfare while outlawing investments in reckless industries like gaming, alcohol, and adult entertainment as well as risky financial products like the derivative contracts that caused the sub-prime crisis in 2008. According to the Pew Research Centre (2021), "India has about 177 million Muslims living there in 2010, making it the third-largest Muslim nation in the world. Many Indian Muslims invest in accounts that don't pay interest or give the interest from interest-bearing accounts to charity". Islamic Banks have a chance to attract capital in a way that traditional banks cannot. Indians have historically engaged in participatory banking through the development of cooperative banks, non-banking financial institutions, and microcredit initiatives".

IFB can be introduced using the same platform. The estimation by Planning Commission about India was to find $300 billion, or 30% additional investment to achieve its infrastructure needs through 2017. "India could use Islamic financial products like *Sukuk* (long-term bonds) to finance infrastructure and other industries, following the lead of nations like Malaysia, Indonesia, the UK, France, and Germany. In particular, **IFB** and finance, which is exclusively intended for Muslims, could draw the Middle East's huge investible surplus to India. In contrast, 40% of customers of Islamic Banks in Malaysia, UK, and other countries are non-Muslims" (Khadar A. & Aneesh A, 2019).

Raghuram Rajan Committee (2008) in its preliminary report, which was made public on presented a number of suggestions for financial sector reforms, including one that strongly supported **IFB**. According to the Committee, "**IFB** is yet another area that largely falls under the purview of financial infrastructure".

"The use of interest-bearing financial products is forbidden by some religions. Some Indians, including those in the economically disadvantaged strata of society, are prevented from accessing banking products and services due to a lack of **IFB** products (where the return to the investor is tied to the bearing of risk, in accordance with the principles of that faith). This absence also prevents India from accessing significant sources of savings from other nations in the area. While there are certain NBFCs and cooperatives that offer **IFB**, the Committee advises that steps be taken to allow for the delivery of Interest Free Finance on a greater scale, including through the banking system. This is in line with the goals of innovation-driven growth and inclusivity (Khadar A. & Aneesh A, 2019)".

The Committee thought it would be possible to develop a framework for such products without having a negative impact on systemic risk by taking the necessary steps. India presents enormous chances to profit from its Muslim population of over 15%, the second-largest in the world and the highest in a non-Islamic nation. Given that there are over 100 million Muslims in India and that the majority of them seek out **IFB** and financing on the basis of their religious beliefs, the market will be quite huge. It is crucial to emphasize that **IFB** extends its benefits not only to Muslims but also to non-Muslims. It is also possible to have a parallel *Shariah*-based banking system in addition to a traditional one. The majority of these nations began withdrawing their investments from the US and Europe after 9/11 out of concern that their assets might be frozen. The decline in the economies of western nations may also be a factor. Islamic countries are extremely excited about India's expanding economy because of the limitless potential it offers. In reality, the Standard & Poor's BRIC *Shariah* Index includes five Indian companies: "Reliance Industries", "Infosys Technologies", "Wipro", "Tata Motors", and "Satyam Computer Services". If **IFB** is implemented, the inadequate labour capital ratio for unorganised sector employees employed in manufacturing and agriculture might be remedied through equity financing, which could lead to a revolution in our unorganised sector and agriculture. "Vulnerable agricultural and unorganised employees would be better able to compete with those in the formal sector with an improved labor-capital ratio" (Khadar A. & Aneesh A, 2019).

IFB could potentially provide significant financial security for a majority of Indian employees. Given that equity financing allows access to credit without incurring debt, the implementation of **IFB** may encourage political leaders to replace grants and subsidies with equity finance programs facilitated through specialized financial organizations. Self-reliance, a crucial goal, can be better achieved through equity financing, as grants and subsidies may fall short in delivering it. It's essential to note that **IFB** need not be exclusive to a religion-based financial industry; instead, it could be strategically utilized to effectively address various economic challenges. Additionally, the Indian government will undoubtedly benefit diplomatically from the implementation of **IFB** in order to conduct business with countries with a majority of Muslims, particularly in order to draw trillions of dollars in equity financing from the Gulf States. This is particularly significant now that financial giants like Lehman Brothers have collapsed since it represents the western economy's slump and the Indian economy's need for alternate FDI sources. In order to draw in the financial incentives from the Gulf region, India must create a friendly economic climate. Islamic scholars have provided a detailed definition of market instruments as well as specific restrictions on stock market investments. While the majority of nations are now offering **Shariah** compatible investment possibilities, India has not experienced significant growth (Khadar A. & Aneesh A, 2019).

To assess the potential of Islamic investments in the Indian stock market, it is essential to examine stocks that adhere to Islamic Shariah principles. "Out of 6,000 BSE listed companies, approximately 4,200 are **Shariah**-compliant. The market capitalization of these stocks accounts for approximately 61% of the total market capitalization of companies listed on BSE. This figure is higher even when compared with a number of predominantly Islamic countries such as Malaysia, Pakistan and Bahrain. In fact, the growth in the market capitalization of these stocks was more impressive than that of the **Non-Shariah**-compliant stocks. The software, drugs and pharmaceuticals and automobile ancillaries sector were the largest sectors among the **Shariah**-compliant stocks. They constitute about 36% of the total **Shariah**-compliant stocks on NSE. Further on examining the BSE 500 the market capitalization of the 321 **Shariah**-compliant companies hovered between 48% and 50% of the total BSE 500 market capitalization" (Raqeeb A., 2010).

"Another opportunity is mutual fund which is based on 100% equity. These funds are invested in different sectors like IT, automobile, telecommunication and cement. In fact, Tata Mutual Fund made a pioneering attempt when, at the instance of the Barkat and some other Islamic financial group, it launched Tata Core Sector Equity Fund in 1996. This scheme was specially tailored keeping in view the Muslims' inhibition of dealing with interest bearing investments. This scheme surprised many by being able to raise Rs. 230 million from the public. Moreover, large number of Muslims who are considered unworthy of credit by commercial banks would welcome **IFB**. People prefer to put their money in gold or jewellery, which is the worst kind of investment from the economic point of view. Some Islamic societies in India accept deposits and lend money, but can't make a business out of it because of the **Shariah's** prohibition of interest. And they are not able to convert themselves into banks because the government will not permit any form of banking without interest. Some of them have collected crores in Interest Free deposits, but they do not have any avenue to invest that money" (Khadar A. & Aneesh A, 2019).

1.17 Issues with Islamic/Interest Free Banking in India

The following principles regulate banking in India:

1. "Cooperative Societies Act", "Negotiable Instruments Act", "Banking Regulation Act of 1949", "RBI Act of 1934", and "Negotiable Instruments Act of 1961" (Moore, 2009; IFSB, 2006).

2. Several of the mentioned acts starkly contradict the core tenets of **IFB**. Likewise, "Section 21 of the Banking Regulation Act of 1949" mandates the payment of interest on deposits, while "Sections 5(b) and 5(c)" explicitly prohibit investments based on profit-and-loss sharing. Additionally, "Section 8 of the Banking Regulation Act of 1949" explicitly states, "No banking company shall directly or indirectly engage in the buying, selling, or bartering of goods".

3. According to the Income Tax Act of 1961, TDS must be withheld from the interest generated on fixed deposits, although **IFB** profits are handled differently.

4. While commercial banks have the option to borrow funds from other financial institutions or the RBI to address short-term funding needs, Islamic Banks face limitations due to their avoidance of interest-based transactions. This restriction necessitates a robust supervisory infrastructure for Islamic Banks, obligating them to regularly monitor their investments across various businesses, ensuring proper management of investee enterprises.

5. Despite the presence of a few training institutions, the shortage of qualified professionals in **IFB** remains a significant challenge. There exists a gap in understanding **IFB** principles, highlighting the need for banks to proactively educate customers about the benefits. This task is formidable, given that Islamic Deposits, such as **Mudarabah** Deposits, neither guarantee principal nor offer a fixed return. Moreover, when engaging in partnerships with firms, Islamic Banks must diligently ensure that managers uphold their responsibilities and do not seek non-pecuniary advantages at the expense of the firm's well-being.

6. Islamic Banks should establish a monitoring cell to stay informed about the internal operations of their joint venture, but doing so would be extremely expensive given the

amount of data that would need to be monitored about the companies in which they participate.

7. The inference here is that a harmonious collaboration between banks and business proprietors is imperative. **IFB** must institute robust corporate governance, adhering to transparent accounting standards, and conduct meticulous assessments prior to the initiation of Profit Loss Sharing Schemes. This necessitates a cadre of highly qualified professionals.

8. It is observed that the challenge of evaluating a project's profitability often impedes investment financing. Some borrowers hinder the appraisal endeavors of banks by withholding comprehensive details about their business. Nevertheless, universally accepted and reliable methodologies are yet to be devised. Given the reluctance of borrowers to adhere to sound business principles, establishing robust client-bank relationships - an essential prerequisite for effective **IFB** - becomes a formidable task.

9. One of the disincentives from the borrower's perspective is the requirement to divulge financial accounts when opting for Profit Loss Sharing arrangements. However, numerous small-scale entrepreneurs fail to maintain any accounts, let alone accurate ones. In the case of large conglomerates, reluctance to disclose authentic financial records adds another layer of complexity.

10. Another significant roadblock in the way of **IFB** in India will be the pervasive absence of corporate ethics among some business communities.

11. The political ramifications of **IFB** might be enormous. Some groups might object to the label "*Shariah*" and claim that it is anti-Indian, while others might contend that the entire idea of *Shariah* banking would violate the secular foundation of our nation.

12. The segmentation between **IFB** and conventional banking has the potential to be manipulated by vested interests to encourage communal divisions within the finance industry in India. This manipulation may lead to the undesirable consequence of financial segregation within the broader economy.

1.18 Statement of the Problem

The conventional banking system, which is prevalent in India, is characterised by borrowing money from its banking customers at a lower interest rate and loaning it to the borrowing customers at a high interest rate. A large number of banks operating on conventional banking system in India have captured a majority of the population as its customer. But yet another large section of the population mainly residing in rural areas is inclined towards the unorganized or informal sector for its money borrowing needs and other related purposes. "This informal/unorganized sector though illegal but has been in force for a long period of time dating back to the inception of *Zamindari* system in India. Such a system not only exploits the weaker section but is corruptive to the Indian economy" (Ayub, 2002). Therefore, it is essential to solve the problems emerging out of the informal banking system systematically. One such way is to substitute the informal banking system with the **IFB** that operates on profit and loss sharing basis and hence provides an investment opportunity to its customers. Till now there are few countries operating on both the forms of banking but "Malaysia" is one such country that has implemented a dual banking system.

Since conventional banking system is largely debt-based, and allows for risk transfer, while the **IFB** system is based on asset and risk sharing, Therefore substitution of informal banking system mediated by *Mahajans* and *Zamindars* calls for the exploration of the **IFB** system thoroughly and strategically. "This exploration further requires a well-established system of banking operating on interest free system. "Here the role of **IFB** system comes into consideration in which the prohibition of *Riba* (interest) serves the principle of equity because it protects the weaker contracting party in a financial transaction from being exploited financially (Hussain et al., 2015)". In addition, "since the lender and the borrower share in the risk of the project, through profit-and-loss Islamic contracts, both participation and equity principles are preserved" (Zaher & Hassan, 2001). "The prohibition of excessive risk-taking *Gharar* also preserves the borrower from any contract ambiguity or asymmetrical information. In line with the participation and ownership principles of **IFB**, all transactions have to be backed by a real economic transaction that involves a tangible asset" (Beck et al., 2013).

Therefore the potential of **IFB** system in India should be explored to tackle the rising inequalities through the informal banking system and as such it is the banking system should be seen through the lens of **IFB** system. The researcher keeping in mind the above stated problem, focused on identifying the current scenario of Conventional Banking in India (Last one Decade) and investigated that whether current Banks (Private as well as Govt.) will be ready to introduce **IFB** or not if investors are ready to adopt it. Further the researcher also aimed to explore the awareness level of respondents regarding **IFB** and the business potential for the same. The study extended its horizons to assess the impact of religion on investing behavior of consumers and the influence of demographic variables (education, age, gender and occupation) on investing behavior of consumers.

In the light of above discussion the statement of the present study was **"Business Potential of Interest Free Banking in India: A Study with Special Reference to Uttar Pradesh"**.

1.19 Significance and Justification of the Research

The Indian banking system is characterized with the wealth maximization objective operating on interest basis. This conventional banking system works on the ground of taking money from its customers at a low interest rate and giving out loan to the borrowers at high interest rates making profits in the process. Since a large population of India is inclined towards the informal money making institutions which are corruptive in nature which further crops a lot of difficulties for the people and for the overall development of the country as well.

Therefore, there is a significant need to solve these unavoidable ills of the informal banking system. This need itself justified the gist of the present research in which the potential of business in the **IFB** system was explored to provide a substitute for the informal money borrowing and lending system.

This research will help in laying the foundational framework to assess the potential of **IFB** system in India by identifying the current conventional banking scenario of India and the readiness of the private and government sector banks in introducing **IFB** units. Furthermore, the findings of this study can offer pertinent insights for both regulators and practitioners, aiding in the development of the **IFB** system and the establishment of best practices within the banking industry. This, in turn, can contribute to offering a viable alternative to the informal banking system.

1.20 Research Questions

Following research questions were framed to address the problem in the study:

1. What is the awareness level of respondents regarding **IFB**?
2. Whether current banks (Private as well as Govt.) will be ready to introduce **IFB** or not if investors are ready to adopt it?

3. What is the business potential of **IFB** in India?
4. What is the impact of religion on investing behavior of consumers?
5. What is the influence of demographic variables (education, age, gender, occupation and monthly income) on investing behavior of consumers?

1.21 Objectives and Hypotheses

The following objectives along with their respective hypotheses guided the study:

Research Objective 1: To test the Awareness Level of Respondents regarding IFB.

$H_{1.1}$: There is a significant difference between Male and Female Respondents among General Public regarding Awareness Level of IFB.

$H_{1.2}$: There is a significant difference between Government Bank and Private Bank Respondents among Bank Officials regarding Awareness Level of IFB.

Research Objective 2: To identify whether current Banks (Private as well as Govt.) will be ready to introduce IFB or not if investors are ready to adopt it.

$H_{2.1}$: There is a significant impact of Awareness Level on the Acceptability Level of IFB from the perspective of General Public.

$H_{2.2}$: There is a significant impact of Awareness Level on the Acceptability Level of IFB from the perspective of Bank Officials.

$H_{2.3}$: There is a significant difference between Male and Female Respondents among General Public regarding Acceptability Level of IFB.

$H_{2.4}$: There is a significant difference between Government Bank and Private Bank Respondents among Bank Officials regarding Acceptability Level of IFB.

Research Objective 3: To explore the Business Potential of IFB in India.

$H_{3.1}$: There is a significant impact of Awareness Level on Business Potential of IFB from the perspective of General Public.

$H_{3.2}$: There is a significant impact of Awareness Level on Business Potential of IFB from the perspective of Bank Officials.

$H_{3.3}$: There is a significant impact of Acceptability Level on Business Potential of IFB from the perspective of General Public.

$H_{3.4}$: There is a significant impact of Acceptability Level on Business Potential of IFB from the perspective of Bank officials.

$H_{3.5}$: There is a significant difference between Male and Female Respondents among General Public regarding Business Potential of IFB.

$H_{3.6}$: There is a significant difference between Government Bank and Private Bank Respondents among Bank Officials regarding Business Potential of IFB.

Research Objective 4: To identify the impact of Religion on Investing Behavior of Respondents.

$H_{4.1}$: There is a significant difference between Investing Behavior of Respondents and their Religions.

$H_{4.1.1}$: There is a significant difference between Respondents' Investing Behavior and their Religion regarding variable that emphasizes on social activities.

$H_{4.1.2}$: There is a significant difference between Respondents' Investing Behavior and their Religion regarding variable that works on the principle of Prohibition of excessive risk/uncertainty.

$H_{4.1.3}$: There is a significant difference between Respondents' Investing Behavior and their Religion regarding variable that only allows the transactions that are backed by a tangible asset.

$H_{4.1.4}$: There is a significant difference between Respondents' Investing Behavior and their Religion regarding variable that does not approve financing of alcohol.

$H_{4.1.5}$: There is a significant difference between Respondents' Investing Behavior and their Religion regarding variable that does not approve financing of pork.

$H_{4.1.6}$: There is a significant difference between Respondents' Investing Behavior and their Religion regarding variable that does not approve financing of ammunitions.

Research Objective 5: To identify the influence of demographic variables (Age, Gender, Educational Qualifications, Occupation and Monthly Income) on Investing Behavior of Respondents.

H_5: There is a significant difference between Respondents' Investing Behavior and their demographic variables (Age, Gender, Education, Occupation and Monthly Income).

$H_{5.1}$: There is a significant difference between Respondents' Investing Behavior and their Age.

$H_{5.1.1}$: There is a significant difference between Respondents' Investing Behavior and their Age regarding variable- Tobacco/Alcohol products.

$H_{5.1.2}$: There is a significant difference between Respondents' Investing Behavior and their Age regarding variable- All Non-Vegetarian Products.

$H_{5.1.3}$: There is a significant difference between Respondents' Investing Behavior and their Age regarding variable- Arms and Ammunition.

$H_{5.1.4}$: There is a significant difference between Respondents' Investing Behavior and their Age regarding variable- Non-Environment Friendly Products.

$H_{5.1.5}$: There is a significant difference between Respondents' Investing Behavior and their Age regarding variable- Products that involves animal cruelty.

$H_{5.2}$: There is a significant difference between Respondents' Investing Behavior and their Gender.

$H_{5.2.1}$: There is a significant difference between Respondents' Investing Behavior and their Gender regarding variable- Tobacco/Alcohol products.

$H_{5.2.2}$: There is a significant difference between Respondents' Investing Behavior and their Gender regarding variable- All non-vegetarian Products.

$H_{5.2.3}$: There is a significant difference between Respondents' Investing Behavior and their Gender regarding variable- Arms and Ammunition.

$H_{5.2.4}$: There is a significant difference between Respondents' Investing Behavior and their Gender regarding variable- Non-Environment Friendly Products.

$H_{5.2.5}$: There is a significant difference between Respondents' Investing Behavior and their Gender regarding variable- Products that involves Animal Cruelty.

$H_{5.3}$: There is a significant difference between Respondents' Investing Behavior and their Educational Qualifications.

$H_{5.3.1}$: There is a significant difference between Respondents' Investing Behavior and their Educational Qualifications regarding variable- Tobacco/Alcohol products.

$H_{5.3.2}$: There is a significant difference between Respondents' Investing Behavior and their Educational Qualifications regarding variable- All non-vegetarian Products.

$H_{5.3.3}$: There is a significant difference between Respondents' Investing Behavior and their Educational Qualifications regarding variable- Arms and Ammunition.

$H_{5.3.4}$: There is a significant difference between Respondents' Investing Behavior and their Educational Qualifications regarding variable- Non-Environment Friendly Products.

$H_{5.3.5}$: There is a significant difference between Respondents' Investing Behavior and their Educational Qualifications regarding variable- Products that involves animal cruelty.

$H_{5.4}$: There is a significant difference between Respondents' Investing Behavior and their Occupation.

$H_{5.4.1}$: There is a significant difference between Respondents' Investing Behavior and their Occupation regarding variable- Tobacco/Alcohol products.

$H_{5.4.2}$: There is a significant difference between Respondents' Investing Behavior and their Occupation regarding variable- All non-vegetarian Products.

$H_{5.4.3}$: There is a significant difference between Respondents' Investing Behavior and their Occupation regarding variable- Arms and Ammunition.

$H_{5.4.4}$: There is a significant difference between Respondents' Investing Behavior and their Occupation regarding variable- Non-Environment Friendly Products.

$H_{5.4.5}$: There is a significant difference between Respondents' Investing Behavior and their Occupation regarding variable- Products that involves animal cruelty.

$H_{5.5}$: There is a significant difference between Respondents' Investing Behavior and their Monthly Income.

$H_{5.5.1}$: There is a significant difference between Respondents' Investing Behavior and their Monthly Income regarding variable- Tobacco/Alcohol products.

$H_{5.5.2}$: There is a significant difference between Respondents' Investing Behavior and their Monthly Income regarding variable- All non-vegetarian Products.

$H_{5.5.3}$: There is a significant difference between Respondents' Investing Behavior and their Monthly Income regarding variable- Arms and Ammunition.

$H_{5.5.4}$: There is a significant difference between Respondents' Investing Behavior and their Monthly Income regarding variable- Non-Environment Friendly Products.

$H_{5.5.5}$: There is a significant difference between Respondents' Investing Behavior and their Monthly Income regarding variable- Products that involves animal cruelty.

1.22 Definition of Terms

- *"Shariah*- is an Islamic canonical law based on the teachings of the *Quran* and the traditions of the Prophet (*Hadith and Sunnah*), prescribing both religious and secular duties and sometimes retributive penalties for lawbreaking. It has generally been supplemented by legislation adapted to the conditions of the day, though the manner in which it should be applied in modern states is a subject of dispute between Muslim traditionalists and reformists" (Ginena & Hamid, 2015).

- *"Gharar-* is an Arabic word that is associated with uncertainty, deception, and risk. It has been described as "the sale of what is not yet present," such as crops not yet harvested or fish not yet netted" (IFSB,2009).

- *"Musharakah-* is a joint enterprise or partnership structure in Islamic finance in which partners share the profits and losses of an enterprise" (Mehtab, Zaheer & Ali, 2015).

- *"Mudarabah-* is a trust based financing agreement whereby an investor (Islamic Bank), entrusts capital to an agent (*Mudarib*) for a project. Profits are based on a prearranged and agreed on ratio" (Gunputh, 2014).

- *"Murabahah-* also referred to as cost-plus financing, is an Islamic financing structure in which the seller and buyer agree to the cost and markup of an asset" (Shahid, Hassan & Rizwan, 2015).

- *"Bai al Salam-* A sale contract for the future production or delivery of commodities, the *Bai al Salam* defines goods and fixes the date of delivery" (IFSB, 2009).

- *"Istisna'a-* refers to a contract for the acquisition of goods by specification where the price is paid at the time of contract, or paid gradually in accordance with the progress or on completion of a job" (IFSB, 2009).

- *"Ijara-* is to give something on rent or providing services and goods temporarily for a wage, it is a term of *Fiqh* (Islamic jurisprudence) and product in **IFB** and finance" (Chhapra, Ahmed, Rehan & Hussain, 2018).

- *"Riba-* can be roughly translated as "usury", or unjust, exploitative gains made in trade or business under Islamic law. *Riba* is mentioned and condemned in several different verses in the Qur'an (3:130, 4:161, 30:39 and most commonly in 2:275-2:280)" (Chong & Liu, 2008).

1.23 Book Framework

The present book on the topic-"**Business Potential of Interest Free Banking in India: A Study with Special Reference to Uttar Pradesh**" is organized under following chapters. Each chapter is a building block to the whole study, the brief description of which is as follows-

- **Chapter 1: Introduction-** The first chapter of the study brings in light the overview of the research on the topic of the study and introduces the statement of the problem.

After the problem statement, important concepts related to the topic are discussed followed by the research questions and the objectives of the research. Then the definitions of the terms along with the justification, need and significance of the study were provided in this chapter. Finally, the organization of the study is discussed in a concise way.

- **Chapter 2: Literature Review-** The second chapter is devoted to the previous researches conducted on the topic of the study to better understand the topic, extract variables for the study, comprehend the methodology used and identify the research gap to work on in this study.

- **Chapter 3: Research Methodology-** The third chapter reveals the hypotheses of the study and is aimed at underlying the research design of the study; determine the type of data source to be used and its collecting method. Apart from it, the sample size determination, sampling technique used, statistical tests, software used and the ethical issues are discussed thoroughly.

- **Chapter 4: Data Analysis and Interpretation-** The fourth chapter is dedicated to the analysis of the data and its interpretation to completely fulfill the objectives of the study.

- **Chapter 5: Findings, Conclusion & Suggestions-** The fifth chapter summarizes the results of the data in concise findings and then concludes it followed by the suggestions in accordance with the results and conclusion of the study. Lastly, the limitations of the research along with the future scope of the study were discussed briefly.

CHAPTER 2: LITERATURE REVIEW

The Literature Review section focuses on prior studies and discoveries related to the topic, aiding in expanding the researcher's knowledge base, identifying key variables, and understanding the methodology used in relevant studies. This chapter is beneficial for research as it helps in expanding the researcher's knowledge base, identifying clustered variables, and comprehending the methodology used in relevant studies.

2.1 Concept of Interest Free Banking

According to Ariss (2010), "**IFB** is based on *Shariah* and permits goods that do not entail *Riba* (interest/usury), *Gharar* (uncertainty), *Maisir* (gambling), and non-*Halal* (prohibited) activities. Islam has permitted profits, but it does not permit returns that are fixed at a certain sum. To receive returns, one must be willing to accept loss risk and profit fluctuation".

Abdel-Haq & Al-Omar (1996) defined *Riba* as "the unjustified earning or receiving of any financial advantage in a business transaction without giving a just counter value".

"When Islamic bonds (*Sukuk*) and hedge funds were first brought to the market, the main products of Islamic Banks were based on simple profit and loss sharing accounts, Islamic savings and investment goods, but now they are flourishing" (Hussain et al., 2015)-

- Profit and loss sharing principle (*Mudarabah*),
- Partnerships or joint ventures (*Musharakah*),
- Sales contract (*Salam*),
- Leasing contract (*Ijara*),
- Interest-free loans (*Qard al Hasan*),
- Trade with markup (*Murabahah*).

2.2 Interest Free Banking: Underlying Principles

According to Hussain et al. (2015), "Islamic Banks adhere to the following moral standards:

- Equity
- Participation
- *Shariah* law's inclusion of ownership"

Interest Free Banking therefore forbids:

- Usury, commonly understood as interest or excessive interest, is referred to as *Riba*.
- Risk or uncertainty, which is often construed as conjecture, is known as *Gharar*, and
- Financing of activities prohibited by *Shariah*, such as the sale of alcohol, pork, and drugs.

According to Hussain et al. (2015), "the prohibition of *Riba* guards the financial exploitation of the weaker contracting party in a financial transaction".

According to Zaher & Hassan (2001), "participation and equity principles are upheld in **IFB** because the lender and borrower share project risk through Islamic profit-and-loss contracts".

Beck et al. (2013) claim that *Gharar's* ban on excessive risk-taking also protects the borrower from any contract ambiguity or information asymmetry. Therefore, each transaction must be supported by a genuine economic transaction involving a physical asset.

2.3 Different Interest Free Banking Products

"Ijara: This product is typically used to buy cars, delivery vans, and other types of vehicles. The bank buys the vehicle for the client, who then pays monthly rentals. Ownership of the vehicle is given to the client upon payment of the vehicle's purchase price plus the profit" (Chhapra, Ahmed, Rehan & Hussain, 2018).

"Mudarabah: This item is utilised in business financing. The bank supplies the money, and the company supplies the labour. If a loss occurs, the bank is responsible for paying it, so long as the *Mudarib* did not intend for it to happen" (Gunputh, 2014).

"Murabahah: This is an agreement to resell things for a profit over their cost. The customer gives the bank the go-ahead to buy the products from a third party. Then, the bank sells the products to the customer for a price that includes both cost and profit. The firm also finances itself using this product" (Shahid, Hassan & Rizwan, 2015).

"Musharakah: This is a partnership contract between the bank and the client wherein both parties commit a specific amount of funds to the enterprise. The partners split the gain or loss in accordance to how much of their capital they contributed, but the gain is divided by agreement in a predetermined ratio" (Mehtab, Zaheer & Ali, 2015).

Around the world, researchers including Abdul-Majid, Saal, & Battisti (2010), Saif-Alyousfi, Saha & Md-Rus (2017), and Samad (2004) looked into the performance disparities between Interest Free and Conventional banking.

According to Ibrahim & Seoweng (2006), "only **IFB** is permitted in Iran, Pakistan, and Sudan. In 2006, it was projected that the global **IFB** and finance market was worth $200 billion to $500 billion USD".

According to Saidi (2007), "Chong & Liu (2008) **IFB** is expanding at an average pace of 15% per year, making it the fastest-growing industry in the financial markets". Similarly in the research of Ghannadian & Goswami (2004), "**IFB** had faster growth than conventional banking". "The size and quantity of Islamic Banks have increased globally, according to Aggarwal & Tarik Yousef" (2000), and are typically the result of private initiatives.

2.4 Consumer Perspective of Interest Free Banking

According to Eriksson (2008), "Customers' preferences and demands must be the primary focus of attention in the banking system".

Har, K.Y. & Ta, H.P. (2000) stated that "bank managers need to learn how to identify the crucial bank selection criteria for the market segments they aim to target and serve".

The extent to which clients employ Islamic banking products and services was evaluated by Naser & Al-Khatib in 1999.

Metawa (1998) investigated "target markets' conduct, attitudes, and perceptions. In order to accomplish their goals, Interest Free Banks need to be aware of their customers' attitudes".

Dusuki & Abdullah (2007) discovered that "choosing **IFB** institutions or services is not solely based on religious motive. Additionally they recognised the following crucial criteria for choosing certain Islamic Banks:

- Cost
- Benefits
- Effective and quick service delivery
- The bank's size and reputation
- Convenience and accessibility (such as location and plenty of parking)
- Friendly nature of bank employees"

According to (Funfgeld & Wang, 2009), "Islamic banks need to comprehend their clients and make their services and goods simply accessible".

According to McCawley (2004), "clients want adequate *Shariah* banking facilities because they fear that traditional banks will mishandle their money".

2.5 Differences between Interest Free and Conventional Banking

Ghannadian & Goswami (2004) highlighted the following "distinctions between **Interest Free Banking** and **Conventional Banking**:

Interest Free Banking-

- Islamic finance excludes interest
- It is based on the tenets of religious convictions

Conventional Banking-

- It is the mainstream banking
- Based on economics concepts"

According to Dusuki & Abdullah (2007) "**IFBs'** fundamental operating tenet is that lending money should be done without charging interest. **IFB** principles hold that the practice of charging interest in the traditional banking system is unfair to borrowers. Instead of charging interest, it mandates that Islamic Banks finance investment projects through profit and loss sharing. While in traditional banking, interest on loans must be paid regardless of how well a company does financially".

Patel (2006) found "equity creation, sharing in profits and losses and rental revenue as prominent characteristics of **IFB** and also added that interest from debt is a factor in conventional banking. The primary distinction between traditional and **IFB** is that in an endeavour, both the banker and the borrower are exposed to risk. **IFB** opposes any form of profit-making that endangers stakeholders or infringes on religious law".

According to Dusuki & Abdullah (2007), "**IFB** is based on the principles of brotherhood and cooperation, which stand for an equality and risk-sharing system. **IFB** does not involve investing money in the creation of -

- Ammunitions
- Tobacco and Alcohol
- Obscene marketing
- Abuse of Animals"

IFB is separated from conventional banking by Chong & Liu (2008) on the basis of the latter's prohibition of *Riba* (interest). Both offer a set rate of return on deposits and adding interest to loans are banned for IBs.

According to Abdel-Haq & Al-Omar (1996), "In **IFB** interest of any kind and Interest-bearing money for consumption or investment purposes is not permitted. Also money is not regarded by *Shariah* as a commodity that has a price attached to it".

According to Saini Y, Bick G, & Abdulla L (2011), "**IFB** permits interest-free loans for charitable endeavours, trade, and investment with profit-and-loss sharing. In **IFB**, trading-related growth is encouraged, while interest-related growth is not allowed. Economic practices that are morally and socially destructive are forbidden in **IFB**. These laws are in line with Islamic teachings that encourage the development of an economic system devoid of any kind of exploitation".

The researchers have discovered that the **IFB** system has gained widespread acceptance on a national scale within the economy. Numerous Muslim nations, such as Bahrain, Dubai, Kuwait, Saudi Arabia, and Malaysia, have implemented a dual system that incorporates both interest-based and **IFB**. In addition to this, Interest Free Banks and investment organizations have been established in Muslim-majority countries like the UK, Denmark, USA, Australia, Singapore, and South Africa. Furthermore, certain interest-based banks have begun providing **IFB** services.

According to Chapra (1986) and Ali (1993), "**IFB** promotes equity between investors and business owners".

In their study, Chong & Liu (2008) found that "Islamic Banks must exert more effort to discern between good and bad clients since they have more to lose than conventional banks and must actively monitor their investments and borrowers".

2.6 Determinants of Bank Selection

Abratt & Russell (1999) determined that "pricing structure for services; service excellence, changing expenses and referrals from friends for banks were the primary variables influencing bank selection. They also found that Price, trust, service quality and the bank's accessibility were the key determinants to ascertain the consumer's criteria for selecting a private bank".

According to Gerrard & Cunningham (1997), "security, variety of services and accessibility of E-services are the most crucial considerations in choosing a bank".

"Family and friend recommendations were determined to be the least essential of the elements" backing banks by Saunders et al. (2007), while the following were considered to be the most crucial:

- Pleasantness of bank employees
- Distance from home
- Reasonable service fees
- Effective and prompt services
- Having conversations with the bank management
- Speed of transactions

According to Tank & Tyler (2005), "the most crucial factors in choosing a bank are the bank's internet websites, referrals from friends and family, and the bank's reputation".

Blackson et al. (2007) identified "Convenience, competence, banking without paying bank fees and peer recommendation as the most crucial ones to consider when choosing a bank".

Amin (2008) found "One of the most crucial factors in choosing a bank was the provision of quick and efficient services".

According to Srivatsa & Srinivasan (2008), "Convenience, web-based banking and accessibility to ATMs were the factors influence customers' bank selections".

According to Dusuki & Abdullah (2007), "Islamic Banks should place a strong emphasis on the effectiveness and quality of their goods and services".

2.7 *Shariah* Governance

Ginena & Hamid (2015) reported that "the term "*Shariah* governance" was introduced in 2003 by M. A. Qatan in his statement, the *Shariah* governance process is a unique building block of the Islamic financial architecture". Later, this idea was used to describe the governance of *Shariah*-compliance in IFIs through standard-setting organisations like Accounting and Auditing Organisation for Islamic Financial Institutions (AAOIFI) and the Islamic Financial Service Board (IFSB)".

The *Shariah* governance system is specifically described by the IFSB (2009) as "a set of institutional and organisational arrangements through which IFIs ensure that there is effective independent oversight of *Shariah*-compliance over the issuance of relevant *Shariah* pronouncements/resolutions and its dissemination, as well as an internal and annual *Shariah*-compliance review/audit".

"Hasan (2012) asserted that "the *Shariah* governance system in IFIs entails a structured mechanism and procedure that call for the participation and coordination of numerous governance organs".

"Numerous researches have looked into corporate governance practices in IBs recently, especially the *Shariah* governance framework". Alkhamees (2013), Grassa (2013, 2015), and (Hasan, 2014) identified "some weaknesses in the existing regulatory frameworks, including ambiguity regarding the roles, responsibilities, and attributes of the *Shariah* Supervisory Board (SSB), both at the national and institutional levels, the competency and independence of the SSB, and the absence of a thorough regulatory framework".

"A governance framework for IBs is lacking, as seen by the wide differences in *Shariah* governance practices across jurisdictions" documented by Grassa & Matoussi (2014), Hasan (2011) and Al Mannai & Ahmed (2018).

Furthermore, studies that analyse the effects of SSB efficacy on bank profitability and value have dominated research about corporate governance in IBs, which calls for further strengthening and standardizing *Shariah* standards. For instance, Ali & Azmi, Grassa, and Kusuma & Ayumardani (2016) "investigated the relationship between corporate governance systems and the traits of IBs, as well as their impact on bank performance".

According to Ghayad (2008), "the performance of a traditional bank and that of an IB, however, should not be compared due to variations in their objectives". Moreover, a number of researches have connected the SSB with earnings management, with varied results, including Elghuweel, Ntim, Opong & Avison (2017), Kolsi & Grassa (2017) and Mersni & Othman (2016).

Furthermore, Mollah & Karim (2011) investigated "whether an IB with a multi-layer governance structure and the SSB in its system avoided collapse during the financial crisis. They discovered that the governance model of IBs provided better protection against the financial crisis since the IBs' restriction of interest had prohibited them from engaging in innovative derivative products and transactions, resulting in less risky assets".

2.8 Impact of Islamic Finance

"The differences between conventional and Islamic Banks are smaller than expected in terms of business model, efficiency, asset quality, or stability, but they find that the share of Islamic Banks in a country significantly affects conventional banks in that country" (Beck et al. 2013).

Beck et al. (2013) gathered data from a sample of 2,956 banks, including 99 Islamic Banks, across 141 countries during the period of 1995-2007. Their findings indicate that an increasing proportion of Islamic Banks correlates with more cost-effective operations but also with reduced stability for traditional banks. According to this report, "Islamic Banks have less market strength than conventional banks, making it necessary for them to engage in successful competition with their traditional counterparts. **IFB** has a variety of effects on the development of the financial industry".

According to McKinsey & Company (2005), "IB must provide them with the needed 'peace of mind' if it hopes to boost the involvement in the banking system from 'unbanked' people who declined to engage in the traditional banking system. **IFB** could lead to financial innovation; encourage the creation of fresh financial products, meeting the demands of investors, borrowers, or depositors. Islamic Banks exert pressure on other banks to do the same in order to maintain their competitive position (the 'spillover effect')".

Empirical studies from Weill (2011) and Beck et al. (2013) provided "proof of how **IFB** affects the strength or cost-effectiveness of the banking sector".

According to Schoon. N. (2016), "the fundamental goal of the *Riba* ban, which forbids lending money to those in need, is to stop wealthy people from abusing the freedom of the poor and the needy".

2.9 Potential of Interest Free Banking

According to Saleem (2008), **IFB** offers the ability to offer loans to people with poor credit ratings and no access to securities. It also has the ability to lower the skyrocketing inflation by reducing the generation of false money and the backing of speculative firms.

"According to Mathews et al. (2004), the ideas of sharing risks and benefits as well as shared participation in wealth creation through equity financing by investors and entrepreneurs, have the ability to foster creativity and productivity in an economy. Furthermore, profit-sharing agreements encourage equity and subsequently generate value for all parties involved".

To ensure that "unbanked" communities excluded by the current financial system are able to access financial services, Indian and foreign institutions must take advantage of Interest Free Baking's untapped potential. The foundation of **IFB** is the idea of maintaining a stable interest rate. **IFB** is available in more than 60 nations globally, and according to research the sector of Islamic finance is still expanding and becoming more sophisticated.

According to H. Mohamed, H Ali, (2019), **IFB** presents a good chance for Indian/foreign banks to increase their presence in India by entering this relatively untouched market. The Indian banking and financial sector can benefit from the addition of an Islamic equity-based banking system. Islamic finance will offer Indian consumers an alternate way to suit their banking demands.

Raqeeb, H. A. (2009) discovered that "the introduction of **IFB** could result in a revolution in India's unorganised agriculture and manufacturing industries by using equity financing to address the inadequate labour capital ratio for workers in these sectors. "With improved labour capital ratio, our vulnerable workers associated with agriculture and the unorganised sector might be able to compete effectively with the workers in the formal sector. Therefore, **IFB** may financially empower the majority of Indian workers". He also claimed that there is a misperception that **IFB** is advantageous just to Muslims and not to everyone.

2.10 Challenges in the Growth of Interest Free Banking

According to IFSB (2009), "the main issues limiting the expansion of **IFB** were the lack of established rules regarding the following-

1. Prudent Techniques
2. Supervision Techniques
3. Accountancy Procedures
4. Auditing Techniques
5. Additional Regulatory Corporate Practices"

"Comparing financial statements published by Islamic financial institutions and those of conventional financial organisations was extremely challenging due to ineffective accounting rules" (IFSB, 2009).

According to Khan & Ahmed (2001), "the lack of standardized contracts and the absence of litigation processes to address issues with the counterparty's ability to enforce contracts, raises the legal risks connected with Islamic contractual relationships".

According to Raqeeb, H. A. (2009), "a proper Indian terminology can be given to the **IFB** system. Nomenclature of Islamic Banking is still a source of worry for regulators and policy makers".

Reserve Bank of India (2014) recommended 'Participatory Banking' in the technical analysis of its interdepartmental report.

2.11 Shortcomings of Islamic Financial Institutions

Islamic institutions are only partially covered, and there is no differentiation made between the different financial sectors (for example, investment banks, wholesale banks, or retail banks are all taken into account equally).

According to Daher et al. (2015), "monitoring complexity issues may exacerbate moral hazard and adverse selection issues. Additionally the research also found that IBs protect shareholders by lessening the effects of displaced commercial risk through stronger capital buffers".

According to Chapra & Ahmed (2002), Iqbal & Mirakhor (2004) and Rahman et al. (2014), "the **IFB** governance model ought to be based on Stakeholders-focused methodology and protect the rights of all parties, whether or not they are stakeholders".

According to Hamza (2016), "in a dual financial system, the existence of fiercely competitive conventional banks, the lack of benchmark pricing for Islamic Bank products, and the immaturity of Islamic money markets cause Islamic Banks' behavior in terms of debt financing to be greatly influenced by changes in monetary policy and conventional bank activity".

- The system of Islamic banks is expected to restrict the ability of monetary policy to affect their debt financing, making **IFB** less efficient.
- Profit Sharing Investment Accounts (PSIA) is a tool used by Islamic Banks to regulate the level of debt financing.
- Islamic Banks use sources of finance to better manage their liquidity, meet demand for debt financing, and improve their compliance with capital adequacy regulations.
- Additionally, Islamic Banks are constantly exposed to the risk of PSIA returns that differ from expectations.
- Displaced Commercial Risk provides traditional banks with a competitive edge.

According to research by Kader & Leong (2009), Sukmana & Kassim (2010), Ergeç & Arslan (2013), Arshad et al. (2015) and Akhatova et al. (2016), "the variation in interest rates can result in deposits moving from Islamic Banks to Conventional Banks due to a 'profit motive' as opposed to a '*Shariah* Motive' which would reduce the level of deposits and probably reduce the volume of debt financing".

According to Rosly (1999), "because Islamic Banks mostly rely on fixed-rate asset financing, which could have a negative impact on their profitability, interest rate changes have a negative impact on their deposits, exposing them to negative fund gaps".

The results of Bacha (2004), Chong & Liu (2009), Zainol & Kassim (2010), Cevik & Charap (2011) and Anuar et al. (2014) demonstrated that "the size and benchmark pricing of PSIA depend on the level and variance of the interest rate on conventional deposits".

"A steady increase in PSIA could strengthen Islamic banks' capitalization and their ability to withstand the negative effects of interest rates", claimed (Hamza & Saddaoui, 2013).

El Hamiani Khatat (2016) claimed that "in the presence of substantial Islamic Banks, the response of Islamic Banks to monetary policy may be effective, resulting in reduced volatility in debt financing".

According to Akhatova et al. (2016) "despite being relatively small in size, Islamic Banks may be more vulnerable to monetary shocks". According to Kahf & Hamadi (2014) "Islamic Banks are predicted to have higher asset liquidity than Conventional Banks". The lack of interest rate-based liquidity management tools and the underdeveloped or incompletely *Shariah*-compliant Islamic products are to blame for the surplus liquidity.

2.12 SWOT Analysis of Interest Free Banking

The SWOT analysis of IFB presents a nuanced perspective on its internal Strengths and Weaknesses, along with external Opportunities and Threats. The strengths of **IFB** lie in its debt-free nature, alignment with social justice principles, a diverse range of financial products, a niche market focus, and its contribution to financial inclusion. Additionally, it serves as a bridge to address rising income disparity. However, weaknesses include the absence of standardized norms, a shortage of experts, the need for modifications in banking regulations, and a prevailing lack of awareness. Opportunities for **IFB** include a sizable Muslim population, potential funds from Gulf countries, and the potential for inclusive growth. On the flip side, "threats include the possibility of being perceived as a political weapon, competition from conventional banking institutions, rivalry from microfinance, and the potential to destabilize the secular nature of the nation (Wulandari S Y et al. 2020)". This comprehensive analysis sheds light on the multifaceted landscape of **IFB**.

SWOT Analysis of IFB	
STRENGTHS	**WEAKNESSES**
• Debt free	• Lack of standardized norms
• Consistent with social justice	• Lack of experts
• Wide financial products	• Modification in Banking Regulation Act needed
• Niche Market	
• Financial inclusion	• Unawareness
• Bridges the rising income disparity	
OPPORTUNITIES	**THREATS**
• Large Muslims Population	• May be projected as a Political Weapon

• Funds from Gulf countries • Inclusive growth	• Competition from conventional banking • Micro finance as competitor • Destabilize Secular Nature of the nation

2.13 International Studies: Islamic Finance

In a case study Bashir (1999) looked at "the relationship between the size of the Islamic Bank (independent variable) and the profitability and market valuation of the Islamic Banks". According to the findings, any bank's profitability is positively and significantly correlated with its size (or scale of operations). Additionally, as scale increases, dangers are reduced and efficiency is increased. However, as the size of operations in Islamic banks grow the market valuation declines.

In order to identify the factors that affect the Middle Eastern Islamic Banks' profitability, Hassan & Bashir (2003) performed study. "For six years (1993–1998), the performance indicators of Islamic banks in eight different countries were tracked. High capital-to-asset and loan-to-asset ratios are associated with higher profitability, according to the study's findings, which also control for taxation, the macroeconomic environment, and the structure of the financial markets. Leaving everything else the same, implicit and explicit taxes have a detrimental impact on the bank's performance and profitability, and the association was notably strong". Government policies also have a significant impact on how well banks perform. For instance, because of opportunity costs, large reserve levels reduce profitability. The favorable macroeconomic conditions exert a positive influence on key performance metrics, manifesting in heightened GDP per capita and elevated inflation rates. These factors collectively contribute to a substantial enhancement in profitability. In the realm of Islamic Banks, profitability is intricately tied to the proportion of profit shared between the business owner and the bank. This stands in contrast to conventional banks, where the primary determinant of revenue lies in the interest rates imposed on loans.

Nienhaus (1983) developed a financial model to examine profitability and concluded that "Islamic Banks charge borrowers almost as much in profit as Conventional Banks charge in interest. This demonstrates that there is no distinction between the profitability of Conventional and Islamic Banks".

Abdul-Majid, Saal & Battisti (2009) conducted a research on the "impact of **IFB** on the cost efficiency and productivity change of Malaysian commercial banks" and found that "Islamic Banks were less effective than conventional banks because they need more input to produce the desired outputs".

"The effectiveness of Islamic Banks operating in two different types of markets - competitive and monopolistic" - was investigated in a study by Haron (1996). The researcher came to the conclusion that in order to prevent monopolist Islamic banks from taking advantage of depositors, a competitive market should be established in the economy through the introduction of new Islamic Banks. The findings of the study further demonstrated that the profit and loss sharing (PLS) approach was advantageous for both depositors and the bank.

Iraj T. and Kabir M. (2011) investigated "the Islamic finance market and discovered that it now started offering a wide range of goods and has established itself as a significant alternative to traditional banking".

Japanese banks are capitalizing on opportunities to offer interest-free loans, strategically maneuvering around the impact of negative interest rates on deposits at the central bank. The primary beneficiaries of this approach are government entities and affiliated borrowers, as banks eagerly deploy available funds to meet an unprecedented demand. The constrained environment has prompted a government lending official to acknowledge the lack of flexibility in rate-setting, expressing a sense of loss for the era when such decisions demonstrated expertise.

In the context of a weekly Finance Ministry auction, which traditionally generated around 1.05 trillion yen ($9.56 billion) in borrowing, there has been a notable surge. Each session now reaches approximately 15 trillion yen, marking a fourteen-fold increase from the actual borrowed amount. Despite the November transition to a 0% interest rate for successful bids (down from 0.001%), banks persist in engaging in aggressive bidding.

'The banker' (2023) listed the Islamic financial institutions. The below table provides the name of the institution, the country name and whether the institution is a Full Islamic Banks (F) or an Islamic Windows (W).

Top 50 Islamic Financial Institutions in the Year 2023:

Rank	Institution	Country	Full Islamic Banks (F), Islamic Windows (W)
1	Al Rajhi Bank	Saudi Arabia	F
2	Saudi National Bank	Saudi Arabia	W
3	Kuwait Finance House	Kuwait	F
4	Dubai Islamic Bank	UAE	F
5	Maybank	Malaysia	W
6	Saudi British Bank (SABB)	Saudi Arabia	W
7	Alinma Bank	Saudi Arabia	F
8	Qatar Islamic Bank (QIB)	Qatar	F
9	Masraf Al Rayan	Qatar	F
10	Abu Dhabi Islamic Bank	UAE	F
11	Riyad Bank	Saudi Arabia	W
12	CIMB Group	Malaysia	W
13	Arab National Bank	Saudi Arabia	W
14	Bank Albilad	Saudi Arabia	F
15	Banque Saudi Fransi	Saudi Arabia	W
16	Bank AlJazira	Saudi Arabia	F
17	Dukhan Bank	Qatar	F
18	Bank Rakyat	Malaysia	F
19	National Bank of Kuwait	Kuwait	W
20	RHB Bank	Malaysia	W
21	Bank Islam	Malaysia	F
22	Public Bank	Malaysia	W
23	Emirates NBD	UAE	W
24	Bank Mandir	Indonesia	W
25	Ahli United Bank	Bahrain	W
26	Islami Bank Bangladesh	Bangladesh	F
27	Sharjah Islamic Bank	UAE	F
28	Qatar International Islamic Bank (QIIB)	Qatar	F
29	Abu Dhabi Commercial Bank	UAE	W

Rank	Institution	Country	Full Islamic Banks (F), Islamic Windows (W)
30	Kuveyt Turk Katilim Bankasi	Turkey	F
31	AmBank Group	Malaysia	W
32	Malaysia Building Society	Malaysia	W
33	Hong Leong Bank	Malaysia	W
34	Kuwait International Bank	Kuwait	F
35	Meezan Bank	Pakistan	F
36	TC Ziraat Bankasi	Turkey	W
37	First Abu Dhabi Bank	UAE	W
38	Al Salam Bank	Bahrain	F
39	GFH Financial Group	Bahrain	F
40	Bank Islam Brunei Darussalam	Brunei	F
41	Affin Bank	Malaysia	W
42	Turkiye Finans Katilim Bankasi	Turkey	F
43	Jordan Islamic Bank	Jordan	F
44	Bank Muamalat Malaysia	Malaysia	F
45	First Security Islami Bank	Bangladesh	F
46	Ithmaar Bank	Bahrain	F
47	Faisal Islamic Bank of Egypt	Egypt	F
48	Ajman Bank	UAE	F
49	EXIM Bank Bangladesh	Bangladesh	F
50	Al Arafah Islami Bank	Bangladesh	F

2.14 Research Gap

The idea discussed in Islamic *Shariah* (law) regarding conducting business is essentially where the **IFB** system derives from. The conventional banking system, on the other hand, is founded on economic principles, with profit determined by the interest collected from loans. On the other hand, **IFB** systems forbid banks from making certain types of investments that involve *Gharar* (uncertainty), *Maisir* (gambling), and non-*Halal* (illegal) operations. Even if income is permitted, the pre-set fixed amount of returns is not. Consumers and banks must both accept the risk of loss and the fluctuation of profits in order to receive rewards.

Numerous studies on various topics relating to the Islamic financial system have been done. The majority of earlier studies concentrated on comprehending the idea of **IFB**. Most of these studies examined **IFB** from a religious standpoint rather than an economic one. Islamic nations established **IFB** systems in response to the demands of those who view charging interest as forbidden. The traditional banking system in India, which mostly focuses on interest, is thriving since both public sector banks and private sector banks are participating and supported.

In addition, Funfgeld & Wang (2009) argued that it is important to comprehend how clients interact with **IFBs'** services and goods. According to McCawley (2004), people have been waiting for legitimate, legal banking services because they fear that traditional banks may mishandle their funds.

In Indian context there is a lot of room for an **IFB** system because the RBI is also interested in it and refers it as 'participatory banking'. This statement applies to the entire people of India, not just one specific community.

As a result, the researcher made the decision to investigate the **"Business Potential of Interest Free Banking in India: A Study with Special Reference to Uttar Pradesh"**. Based on these two facts, the researcher made an assumption about the viability of an **IFB** system. First, despite having a large population, India still has a large untapped market for the conventional banking system. The second reality is that there is a very diverse population in India.

The business potential of **IFB** in India has not been studied in any studies. Therefore, after carefully reviewing the previously published literature, the researcher decided to look into this. To determine whether current banks (including Private and Government) will be prepared to implement **IFB** or not, if investors are ready to adopt it.

The researcher studied the following aspects of **IFB** system-

- Business potentiality of **IFB** system.
- Readiness of Conventional Banking System for adopting **IFB** system / Participatory Banking System.
- Awareness level of General Public regarding **IFB**.
- Impact of religion on investing behavior of Indian consumers.

- Influence of demographic variables on investing behavior of consumers.

The aforementioned issues must be taken into account as the research gap and the basis for the research. Without regard to its religious component, the researcher investigated the feasibility of an **IFB** system and took into account all other potential points of agreement that will made it acceptable to the individuals. The researcher also took into account the perspectives of General Public as well as Bank Officials.

CHAPTER 3: RESEARCH METHODOLOGY

3.1. Research Design and Methodology

According to N Walliman (2011), "Research can be defined as an activity that involves finding out, in a more or less systematic way, things you did not know". In the opinion of Brown (2006), "Methodology is the philosophical framework within which the research is conducted or the foundation upon which the research is based". O'Leary (2004) described "methodology as the framework that is used to conduct research". According to Remenyi, Williams, Money, & Swartz (1998), "Research Methodology refers to the procedural framework within which research is conducted". Allan and Randy (2005) insisted that "research methodology should meet the following two criteria while conducting a research:

- Methodology must help to achieve research objective.
- It should be replicable".

Research Methodology chapter of a research describes following headings in detail highlighting those used throughout the study -

- Research Methods
- Approaches
- Designs

This chapter delineates the design and execution of the present study. A survey was meticulously crafted to investigate the **exploratory** research topic, **"Business Potential of Interest Free Banking in India: A Study with Special Reference to Uttar Pradesh".** The primary aim of this chapter is to furnish a lucid and all-encompassing description of the specific factors considered in addressing the research problem and hypotheses. Additionally, the chapter expounds on the methodologies employed for the empirical data analysis.

3.2 Research Design

According to Singh, K. (2007), "Descriptive research is aimed at casting light on current issues or problems through a process of data collection that enables them to describe the situation more completely that was not possible without employing this method". This type of research aims to describe the state of affairs as it is without manipulating it. In relation to the present study, the researcher aimed to shed light on the awareness level, acceptability level and business potential of **IFB** in India with special reference to Uttar Pradesh. This aim of the study aligns with the descriptive research.

"Exploratory research is employed to develop initial ideas and insights and to provide direction for any further research needed. An exploratory study is essential when a researcher needs to identify problems, defines the problem more precisely and identifies any specific objectives or data requirements to be addressed through additional research. The exploratory research is highly flexible, unstructured and qualitative. Exploratory research is when a study is undertaken with the objective either to explore an area where little is known or to investigate the possibilities of undertaking a particular research study" (Swaraj. A, 2019). The present study aligns with the exploratory research as it aims to identify whether current Banks (Private as well as Govt.) will be ready to introduce **IFB** or not if investors are ready to adopt it. In addition, the study also explored the impact of Awareness Level & Acceptability Level of **IFB** on Business Potential from the perspective of general public& bank officials.

Another research designs with aligns with the present study is a quantitative method which is usually applied when the purpose is to verify existing theories or test hypotheses. The researcher aims to study the influence of demographic variables (ages, genders, religion, educational qualifications, occupations & monthly income) on investing behavior of consumers and test the hypotheses related to the objectives of the study.

However, the researcher gave depth to the quantitative results of the study by interpreting and concluding it in a qualitative approach to explore the subject matter in detail as a qualitative method is a better way to create understanding in a specific subject. Also, both methods have weak sides, that is why combining the two methods is recommended (Holme & Solvang 1997).

Therefore, in light of the above mentioned research designs, it can be said that the present study has used descriptive, exploratory, qualitative and quantitative research design.

3.3 Data Sources: Primary & Secondary Data

In essence, there are two fundamental types of data sources: primary and secondary.

Primary sources are directly aligned with the study's purpose. It encompasses all data collected throughout the study that is directly pertinent to the research objectives, whether gathered personally or obtained from a third party with a similar research intent. In this study, primary data was procured through an empirical investigation, utilizing two distinct questionnaires tailored for different respondent groups—one for the general public and another for bank officials.

On the other hand, **secondary data** comprises relevant information collected for a different purpose but holds value for the current study. In this research, the researcher obtained secondary data for the literature review exclusively from the official **SCOPUS** database website. This approach ensured that the secondary data sourced was pertinent and contributed effectively to the study's objectives.

In view of the sources of data, the researcher used primary as well as secondary data in the present study.

3.4 Constructs under the Study

1. **Awareness Level (of IFB)**
2. **Acceptability Level (of IFB)**
3. **Business Potential (of IFB)**

3.5 Scale Development

Since, Clark, L. A., & Watson, D. (1995), claimed that scale development is an essential stage in the assessment of constructs and variables in any social science. It helps to develop levels of the constructs. Therefore, to understand the constructs of the study completely with their underlying variables the researcher developed a scale index to decide the overall level of each construct. Before beginning the process of developing level of constructs, the researcher throws light on the conceptualization of the three constructs- Awareness Level, Acceptability Level and Business Potential of **IFB**.

- **Awareness Level of IFB**

In the context of this study, "Awareness Level" refers to the understanding and knowledge individuals (General Public and Bank Officials) have about the concept and operations of **IFBS**. Various variables measure the depth of this awareness. For example, respondents are asked if they are aware of the basic concept of **IFB**, the absence of predetermined returns, the reliance on trading for profits, the acceptance of risk and profit sharing, and the avoidance of the time value of money principle. Additionally, awareness extends to the services provided by IFBS, such as profit and loss sharing, partnerships or joint ventures, sales and leasing contracts, interest-free loans, trade with mark-up, and special types of trading agreements. This set of variables aims to gauge how well general public and bank officials are informed about the fundamental aspects and services associated with **IFB**.

- **Acceptability Level of IFB**

In the context of this study, "Acceptability Level" refers to the willingness of individuals (General Public and Bank Officials) to embrace and support the principles and practices associated with **IFB** (IFB). The acceptability is measured through various criteria that respondents are asked to consider. For instance, participants are queried on their acceptance of banking systems that adhere to principles of participation and equity, eliminate contract ambiguity in favour of tangible asset transactions, prohibit economically and socially harmful activities, incorporate profit and loss sharing, avoid investments in certain industries (like ammunitions, alcohol, tobacco, offensive advertising, and cruelty to animals), eliminate fixed rates of return on deposits, and promote justice and freedom from exploitation in financial dealings. These criteria collectively assess the extent to which General Public and Bank Officials are open to embracing the values and practices inherent in **IFB**.

- **Business Potential of IFB**

In the context of this study, "Business Potential" pertains to the prospects and capabilities of **IFB** as a viable and beneficial banking system. This potential is evaluated through several key considerations that respondents are asked to assess. For instance, participants are queried about their perception of a banking system's potential to provide loans to those without securities, create value for all parties involved, complement the existing Indian banking and finance system, contribute to greater financial inclusion, and support micro and small enterprises. Additionally, the evaluation extends to the potential benefits for both depositors and the bank itself. These criteria collectively gauge the perceived viability and advantages of **IFB** from a business standpoint.

After defining the constructs the researcher studied following number of variables in the dimensions of the study mentioned below in case of General Public and Bank Officials.

Table 3.1- Variables

Dimension	No. of variables in case of General Public	No. of variables in case of Bank Official.
Awareness Level	14	14
Acceptability Level	09	09
Business Potential	21	27
Total	**44**	**50**

3.6 Questionnaire Development and Administration

To comprehensively address the study's objectives, various measures related to the demographic and socio-economic profiles of the respondents, along with other constructs pertinent to the research objectives were carefully considered. This process involved extensive discussions with the research guide, esteemed academicians, expert professors, a thorough literature review, and exploratory investigations.

Following these consultations and examinations, two meticulously designed questionnaires were developed- one for the General Public and another for Bank Officials. These questionnaires were structured with precision to gather pertinent and insightful data, ensuring that the study's objectives were effectively addressed.

Close-ended structured questionnaires were employed to facilitate effective data analysis. As previously mentioned, the items in the questionnaires were crafted from relevant research and thoughtfully adapted for this study. Respondents were prompted to provide their responses to questions pertaining to demographic information. These questions were formulated using a range of close-ended formats, including **objective questions**, dichotomous questions, and **multiple-choice questions** in both questionnaires. This approach allowed for a systematic and quantitative analysis of the collected data.

For the remaining sections of the questionnaires, applicable to both the General Public and Bank Officials, the questions were structured using a five-point Likert scale. The Likert scale ranged from "Strongly Agree (5)" to "Strongly Disagree (1)", with intermediate options including "Agree (4)", "Undecided (neither agree nor disagree) (3)" and "Disagree (2)". Respondents were prompted to express their attitudinal responses by indicating their level of agreement or disagreement with various statements pertaining to the study's topic. This approach enabled a nuanced exploration of participants' perspectives and attitudes through a structured and quantifiable format.

3.7 Pilot Study

Before the pilot study, the questionnaires underwent a thorough review by experts to enhance their face validity and content validity. Consequently, the initial draft of the questionnaire for the General Public, which originally comprised 63 questions, underwent refinement. One question (City) was added for the pilot study, and 8 questions were removed, resulting in a final set of 56 questions used for the pilot study.

Similarly, in the case of the questionnaire for Bank Officials, the initial draft encompassed 65 questions. For the pilot study, 2 questions (City, Type of bank) were added, and 8 questions were removed. The final version of the questionnaire for Bank Officials consisted of 59 questions after this iterative refinement process.

The decision to remove certain questions from the initial questionnaire was grounded in the objective of enhancing validity. Questions were excluded based on the following criteria:

- Questions that duplicated or repeated information were identified and eliminated.
- Questions lacking relevance to the context of the research construct were omitted.
- Any questions that raised concerns regarding research ethics were excluded.

After that, pilot study was conducted with a sample size of **102** respondents (**51 respondents were General Public and 51 respondents were Bank Officials**), to improve the reliability of the data and clarify the overall structure of the final questionnaires. Data for General Public was collected from Mau District of Uttar Pradesh and for Bank Officials from Lucknow. Two separate questionnaires were used for the two groups' of respondents and these respondents were selected using **Convenience-Sampling Method.**

The pilot study helped to finalise Questionnaires, the details of which are as follows-

In case of Questionnaire for General Public- The questions with a Cronbach's alpha value below 0.6 were excluded. Consequently, four questions were eliminated, resulting in a final questionnaire for the General Public comprising 52 questions out of the initial 56.

In case of Questionnaire for Bank Officials- The questions with a Cronbach's alpha value below 0.6 were excluded. As a result, eight questions were omitted, leading to the final questionnaire for Bank Officials consisting of 51 questions from the initial set of 59.

3.8 Sampling Technique, Sample Size and Data Collection

The target population of the present research consisted of the people who were using **banking services** or **aware about it** and those **Bank Officials** who were working in **Government** and **Private Banks** in **Uttar Pradesh, India**. This population was considered as the **realistic/accessible population**. In this research, the sampled population consisted of the people who were using **banking services** or **were aware about it** and those **Bank Officials** who were working in **Government and Private Banks** in the major cities of Uttar Pradesh: **KALAM (Kanpur, Allahabad (Currently Prayagraj) Lucknow, Azamgarh** and **Mau.**

The sample size and respondents from the population were on the basis of the stake the respondents hold in bank i.e. public or the officials and on this basis the entire population was divided into two groups- **General Public and Bank Officials. The planned sample size** of the study for **General Public** was **1500** and for **Bank Officials 500**.

Quota Sampling Technique was used to collect the primary data. This technique is a Non-random Sampling Technique, in which population is divided into groups and then, from each group sample is taken non-randomly.

The **Sample Unit of analysis** was a **person (General Public)** who uses banking services or knows about it and in case of **Bank Officials** the **Sample Unit of analysis** was a **Bank Officials**.

3.8.1 Process of Developing Scale: Administration & Scoring

The scale development process for both the General Public and Bank Officials followed a similar procedure. Initially, the final questionnaires were distributed among the respective respondents. The questionnaire's ultimate version included items where respondents expressed their agreement on a 5-point scale. Each of the variables/items for the General Public and variables/items for Bank Officials were assigned scores ranging from 5 to 1. The choices provided were **"Strongly Agree (5)"**, **"Agree (4)"**, **"Undecided/Neutral (3)"**, **"Disagree (2)"**, **and "Strongly Disagree (1)"**. Respondents were prompted to select the option that best represented their agreement or disagreement with each item, facilitating a systematic and standardized method of data collection.

Researcher developed index for measuring the Awareness Level, Acceptability Level and Business Potential in case of General Public and Bank Officials and performed the following steps-

Z-score Conversion: All scores for each variable were converted into Z-scores. This normalization process allows for a standardized comparison of scores across different variables.

Total Score Calculation: The total score for all the variables within each of the 3 dimensions was computed for each respondent. This provided an overall measure for each dimension.

Class Interval Determination: Class intervals were established based on the range. The range was divided by 5 for both General Public and Bank Officials, facilitating the creation of intervals.

Category Division based on Z-scores: The Z-scores were utilized to categorize respondents. Five categories were determined based on the division of Z-scores. This categorization helped in classifying respondents according to their scores.

Coding: Finally, each of the variables for the General Public Bank Officials were assigned scores ranging from 5 to 1. The lowest value was coded as 1, and the highest value was coded as 5 for both General Public and Bank Officials. This coding system simplified the representation and interpretation of the data.

This methodical approach ensured a structured and standardized analysis of the collected data, allowing for meaningful comparisons and insights.

3.9 Data Collection

In the case of the General Public, a total of **2,200** questionnaires were distributed, and **1,319** filled questionnaires were received, representing a response rate of **59.95%**. Among the received questionnaires, **1,236** were completed and considered usable, resulting in an effective response rate of **56.18%**.

On the other hand, **1,200** questionnaires were administered for data collection from Bank Officials. However, **only 461 filled questionnaires** were received, reflecting a response rate of **38%**. Out of these, **436** were fully completed and considered usable, yielding an **effective response rate of 36.33%.**

Hence, the total **Sample Size** comprised of **1672 respondents (1236 respondents were General Public and 436 respondents were Bank Officials).**

The questionnaires were handed out directly to respondents, from the mid of **February 2023** up till the mid of **April 2023.**

Table 3.2- Sample Size

	General Public	Bank Officials
Planned Sample Size	1500	500
Questionnaire Distributed	2200	1200
Filled Questionnaire Received	1319	461
Complete & Usable Questionnaire	**1236**	**436**

Table 3.3- Distribution of respondents: city wise- In case of General Public

Cities					
		Frequency	Percent	Valid Percent	Cumulative Percent
Valid	Kanpur	144	11.7	11.7	11.7
	Prayagraj	195	15.8	15.8	27.4
	Lucknow	513	41.5	41.5	68.9
	Azamgarh	231	18.7	18.7	87.6
	Mau	153	12.4	12.4	100.0
	Total	1236	100.0	100.0	

Table 3.4- Distribution of respondents: city wise- In case of Bank Officials

Cities					
		Frequency	Percent	Valid Percent	Cumulative Percent
Valid	Kanpur	44	10.1	10.1	10.1
	Prayagraj	59	13.5	13.5	23.6

	Lucknow	215	49.3	49.3	72.9
	Azamgarh	70	16.1	16.1	89.0
	Mau	48	11.0	11.0	100.0
	Total	436	100.0	100.0	

The separate statistical tables in case of both General Public and Bank Officials are provided below:

Table 3.5- Statistics: General Public

Statistics: General Public				
		Awareness Level	Acceptability Level	Business Potential
N	Valid	1236	1236	1236
	Missing	0	0	0
Mean		.0000053	-.0000069	.0000040
Range		37.53359	29.44824	18.70551
Minimum		-19.90193	-16.28011	-11.17103
Maximum		17.63166	13.16813	7.53448
Class Interval		7.5	5.8	3.74
Very Low Level-1		From -19.90 To -12.40	From -16.28 To -10.49	From -11.17 To -7.43
Low Level-2		From -12.39 To -4.89	From -10.48 To -4.68	From -7.42 To -3.67
Moderate Level-3		From -4.87 To 2.58	From -4.67 To 1.11	From -3.66 To 0.03
High Level-4		From 2.59 To 10.10	From 1.12 To 6.91	From 0.04 To 3.78

Very High Level-5	From	From	From
	10.11	6.92	3.79
	To	To	To
	17.64	13.17	7.54

The researcher categorized all dimensions into five distinct levels based on Z-scores, resulting in a conversion of all variables into categorical variables. The categorization is as follows:

- **Very Low Level**
- **Low Level**
- **Moderate Level**
- **High Level**
- **Very High Level**

Table 3.6- Statistics: Bank Officials

Statistics: Bank Officials				
		Awareness Level	Acceptability Level	Business Potential
N	Valid	436	436	436
	Missing	0	0	0
Mean		.0000051	-.0000023	.0000023
Range		34.91732	19.56229	37.45415
Minimum		-16.20440	-10.66634	-21.19050
Maximum		18.71292	8.89595	16.26365
Class Interval		6.98	3.9	7.49
Very Low Level-1		From	From	From
		-16.20	-10.66	-21.19
		To	To	To
		-9.22	-6.76	-13.70
Low Level-2		From	From	From
		-9.21	-6.75	-13.69
		To	To	To
		-2.23	-2.84	-6.20
Moderate Level-3		From	From	From
		-2.22	-2.83	-6.19
		To	To	To

	4.72	1.02	1.26
High Level-4	From 4.73 To 11.71	From 1.03 To 5.01	From 1.27 To 8.76
Very High Level-5	From 11.971 To 18.72	From 5.02 To 9.0	From 8.77 To 16.27

The researcher categorized all dimensions into five distinct levels based on Z-scores, resulting in a conversion of all variables into categorical variables. The categorization is as follows:

- **Very Low Level**
- **Low Level**
- **Moderate Level**
- **High Level**
- **Very High Level**

3.10 Reliability Analysis

Cronbach's Alpha is a widely employed method for investigating the reliability of a scale, often utilized to assess the overall consistency of measurements within the scale.

3.10.1 Reliability Analysis: General Public

Table 3.7- Reliability Statistics

Reliability Statistics			
	Cronbach's Alpha	No. of Items	No. of Respondents
Entire Data	**0.814**	51	1236
Awareness of **IFB** System (IFBS)	**0.693**	14	1236
Acceptability for **IFB** System	**0.669**	9	1236
Business Potential of **IFB** System	**0.839**	6	1236

Interpretation: The value Cronbach's Alpha in case of General Publics' data is very high (0.814) and in case of dimensions- Awareness of **IFB** System (IFBS) is also high (0.693); in case of dimensions- Acceptability for **IFB** System (IFBS) is also high (0.669); and finally in case of dimensions- Business Potential of **IFB** System is also high (0.839). This signifies that the data for entire scale and all dimensions is having high reliability for General Public.

3.10.2 Reliability Analysis: Bank Officials

Table 3.8- Reliability Statistics

Reliability Statistics			
	Cronbach's Alpha	No. of Items	No. of Respondents
Entire Data	0.788	42	436
Awareness of **IFB** System (IFBS)	0.771	12	436
Acceptability for **IFB** System	0.665	8	436
Business Potential of **IFB** System	0.659	10	436

Interpretation: The value Cronbach's Alpha in case of Bank officials' data is very high (0.788) and in case of dimension- Awareness of **IFB** System (IFBS) is also high (0.771); in case of dimension- Acceptability for **IFB** System (IFBS) is also high (0.665); and finally in case of dimension- Business Potential of **IFB** System is also high (0.659). This signifies that the data for entire scale and all dimensions is having high reliability for Bank Officials.

3.11 Descriptive Statistics

3.11.1 Descriptive Statistics: General Public's Data

Table 3.9- Descriptive Statistics: General Public's Data

Descriptive Statistics					
	N	Minimum	Maximum	Mean	Std. Deviation
I am aware of the concept of **IFB** system.	1236	1	5	3.60	1.165
I am aware that **IFB** does not allow pre- determined fix amount of returns.	1236	1	5	3.46	1.043

	N	Mini mum	Maxi mum	Mean	Std. Deviation
I am aware that in **IFB** profits are allowed through trading activity only.	1236	1	5	3.67	.998
I am aware that in **IFB** risk of loss and variability of profits must be faced to get the returns (profit and loss sharing).	1236	1	5	3.44	1.059
I am aware that **IFB** does not believe in time value of money with respect earning profit in form of interest.	1236	1	5	3.55	1.115
I am aware that IFBS does not deal in the products that involve interest.	1236	2	5	3.93	.913
I am aware that pre-determined fix amount of returns is not allowed in IFBS	1236	1	5	3.80	1.013
I am aware that **IFB** has the system of Profit and loss sharing.	1236	1	5	3.66	1.085
I am aware that **IFB** is a kind of Partnerships or joint ventures.	1236	1	5	3.49	1.111
I am aware that **IFB** provides Sales contract.	1236	1	5	3.40	1.089
I am aware that **IFB** provides Leasing contract.	1236	1	5	3.48	1.047
I am aware that **IFB** provides Interest-free loans.	1236	1	5	3.43	1.089
I am aware that **IFB** provides Trade with mark-up.	1236	1	5	3.00	1.234
I am aware that **IFB** provides special type of trading agreement.	1236	1	5	2.94	1.220
Participation and equity principles are preserved.	1236	3	5	4.21	.619
There is Elimination of contract ambiguity and involvement of only real economic transactions having a tangible asset.	1236	1	5	3.50	1.118

	N	Minimum	Maximum	Mean	Std. Deviation
Economic activities that are morally and socially harmful are prohibited.	1236	4	5	4.41	.493
There is profit and loss sharing.	1236	1	5	2.26	.680
There is no investment of funds in the production of- Ammunitions, Alcohol and tobacco, Offensive advertising, Cruelty to animals.	1236	1	5	3.98	.945
There is no fixed rate of return on deposits nor is any interest charged on loans.	1236	1	5	4.09	.884
Increase in return produced by trading is welcomed but by interest is prohibited.	1236	1	5	4.02	.880
There is freedom from all forms of exploitations and there is justice between the financer and the entrepreneur	1236	3	5	4.21	.504
Risk of loss and variability of profits must be faced to get the returns (profit and loss sharing)	1236	1	3	1.90	.654
Potential to provide loans to those who do not have securities at disposal.	1236	1	5	3.63	.981
Potential to create value for each of the contracting parties involved	1236	1	5	3.54	1.237
Potential to complement the existing Indian banking and finance system	1236	2	5	3.77	1.003
Potential to contribute towards greater financial inclusion	1236	3	5	4.23	.628
Potential to support micro and small enterprises.	1236	3	5	4.17	.623
Potential to benefit depositors as well as the bank.	1236	3	5	4.21	.666

	N	Mini mum	Maxi mum	Mean	Std. Deviation
Emphasizes social activities	1236	3	5	4.15	.682
That works on the principle of Prohibition of excessive risk/ uncertainty.	1236	3	5	4.29	.580
Only allows the transactions that are backed by a tangible asset.	1236	1	5	3.30	1.233
Does not approve financing of alcohol.	1236	1	5	3.07	1.234
Does not approve financing of pork.	1236	1	5	2.78	1.656
Does not approve financing of ammunitions	1236	1	5	2.76	1.266
Tobacco/Alcohol products	1236	1	5	3.57	1.111
All non-vegetarian Products	1236	1	5	2.64	1.119
Arms and Ammunition	1236	1	5	2.10	.741
Non-Environment Friendly Products	1236	1	5	3.38	1.227
Products that involves animal cruelty	1236	3	5	4.23	.626
Valid N (list wise)	1236				

3.11.2 Descriptive Statistics: Bank Officials' Data

Table 3.10- Descriptive Statistics: Bank Officials' Data

Descriptive Statistics					
	N	Mini mum	Maxi mum	Mean	Std. Deviation
I am aware of the concept of **IFB** system.	436	1	5	3.33	1.093
The concept of **IFB** system can be implemented in India.	436	1	5	3.22	1.081
I am aware that **IFB** will not allow pre-determined fix amount of returns.	436	1	5	3.43	1.021
I am aware that in **IFB** profits will be allowed through trading activity only.	436	1	5	3.42	1.097

	N	Mini mum	Maxi mum	Mean	Std. Deviation
I am aware that in **IFB**, risk of loss and variability of profits will be faced by stakeholders to get the returns (profit and loss sharing).	436	1	5	3.29	.996
I am aware that **IFB** will not consider time value of money with respect earning profit in form of interest.	436	1	5	3.15	.926
I am aware that IFBS will not deal in the products that involve interest.	436	1	5	3.43	.984
I am aware that **IFB** will be like a Partnership or joint venture.	436	1	5	3.46	1.051
I am aware that **IFB** will provide Sales contract.	436	1	5	3.21	1.059
I am aware that **IFB** will provide Leasing contract.	436	1	5	3.31	1.120
I am aware that **IFB** will provide Interest-free loans.	436	1	5	3.54	1.147
I am aware that **IFB** will provide special type of trading agreement.	436	1	5	3.53	1.121
Participation and equity principles are preserved.	436	1	5	3.42	1.033
There is Elimination of contract ambiguity and involvement of only real economic transactions having a tangible asset.	436	1	5	3.36	.882
Economic activities that are morally and socially harmful are prohibited.	436	1	5	3.82	1.073
There is profit and loss sharing.	436	1	5	3.38	.921
There is no investment of funds in the production of- Ammunitions, Alcohol and tobacco, Offensive advertising, Cruelty to animals.	436	1	5	3.70	.937

	N	Mini mum	Maxi mum	Mean	Std. Deviation
There is no fixed rate of return on deposits nor is any interest charged on loans.	436	1	5	3.54	1.087
There is freedom from all forms of exploitations and there is justice between the financer and the entrepreneur.	436	1	5	3.74	1.040
Risk of loss and variability of profits must be faced to get the returns (profit and loss sharing)	436	1	5	3.36	1.094
IFB System has the business potential in India.	436	1	5	3.26	1.145
The customer base is large enough to start an alternative banking system.	436	1	5	3.22	1.171
With time, customer base of **IFB** can be increased.	436	1	5	3.29	1.067
IFSB should have transparency for business investments.	436	1	5	3.63	.961
IFBS will be able to fulfill needs of depositors, investors and borrowers.	436	1	5	3.03	1.160
IFBS will be a good substitute for informal money lending institutions.	436	1	5	3.73	.963
IFSB will be able to get enough investment.	436	1	5	3.09	1.137
IFBS will be able to gain enough profit.	436	1	5	3.26	1.187
IFBS needs to be governed by any specific regulatory body.	436	1	5	3.55	.964
IFB System can be developed in India for all.	436	1	5	3.53	1.094
Potential to provide loans to those who do not have securities at disposal.	436	1	5	3.67	1.007
Potential to create value for each of the contracting parties involved	436	1	5	3.17	1.073

	N	Minimum	Maximum	Mean	Std. Deviation
Potential to complement the existing Indian banking and finance system	436	1	5	3.31	.996
Potential to contribute towards greater financial inclusion	436	1	5	3.36	1.002
Potential to support micro and small enterprises.	436	1	5	3.36	1.145
Potential to attract consumers from Arab countries.	436	1	5	3.86	1.000
Potential to benefit depositors as well as the bank.	436	1	5	3.21	1.203
Works on the principle of Prohibition of excessive risk/ uncertainty.	436	1	5	2.52	1.117
Allows only the transactions that are backed by a tangible asset.	436	1	5	2.77	1.130
Does not approve financing of alcohol.	436	1	5	3.35	1.120
Does not approve financing of certain or all meat products.	436	1	5	3.65	1.123
Does not approve financing of ammunitions.	436	1	5	3.32	1.152
Valid N (list wise)	436				

3.12 Normalcy Analysis of the Data

To meet the study's objectives, the researcher conducted a normality analysis to assess the distribution of the data. This step was essential for determining whether parametric or non-parametric statistical tests would be more appropriate for subsequent analyses. Since the present study have two set of respondents i.e. general public & bank officials, therefore normalcy analysis was done separately for both cases. The result of which is presented below-

3.12.1 Normalcy Analysis: General Public's Data

Table 3.11- Tests of Normality: General Public

Normality Test			
	Shapiro-Wilk		
	Statistic	df	Sig.
I am aware of the concept of **IFB** system.	.883	1236	.000
I am aware that **IFB** does not allow pre- determined fix amount of returns.	.896	1236	.000
I am aware that in **IFB** profits are allowed through trading activity only.	.859	1236	.000
I am aware that in **IFB** risk of loss and variability of profits must be faced to get the returns (profit and loss sharing).	.900	1236	.000
I am aware that **IFB** does not believe in time value of money with respect earning profit in form of interest.	.882	1236	.000
I am aware that IFBS does not deal in the products that involve interest.	.851	1236	.000
I am aware that pre-determined fix amount of returns is not allowed in IFBS	.873	1236	.000
I am aware that **IFB** has the system of Profit and loss sharing.	.886	1236	.000
I am aware that **IFB** is a kind of Partnerships or joint ventures.	.901	1236	.000
I am aware that **IFB** provides Sales contract.	.905	1236	.000
I am aware that **IFB** provides Leasing contract.	.901	1236	.000
I am aware that **IFB** provides Interest-free loans.	.905	1236	.000
I am aware that **IFB** provides Trade with markup.	.913	1236	.000
I am aware that **IFB** provides special type of trading agreement.	.913	1236	.000
Participation and equity principles are preserved.	.770	1236	.000
There is Elimination of contract ambiguity and	.899	1236	.000

involvement of only real economic transactions having a tangible asset.			
Economic activities that are morally and socially harmful are prohibited.	.626	1236	.000
There is profit and loss sharing.	.589	1236	.000
There is no investment of funds in the production of- Ammunitions, Alcohol and tobacco, Offensive advertising, Cruelty to animals.	.846	1236	.000
There is no fixed rate of return on deposits nor is any interest charged on loans.	.748	1236	.000
Increase in return produced by trading is welcomed but by interest is prohibited.	.758	1236	.000
There is freedom from all forms of exploitations and there is justice between the financer and the entrepreneur	.673	1236	.000
Risk of loss and variability of profits must be faced to get the returns (profit and loss sharing)	.791	1236	.000
Potential to provide loans to those who do not have securities at disposal.	.856	1236	.000
Potential to create value for each of the contracting parties involved	.861	1236	.000
Potential to complement the existing Indian banking and finance system	.828	1236	.000
Potential to contribute towards greater financial inclusion	.773	1236	.000
Potential to support micro and small enterprises.	.774	1236	.000
Potential to benefit depositors as well as the bank.	.788	1236	.000
Emphasizes social activities	.797	1236	.000
That works on the principle of Prohibition of excessive risk/ uncertainty.	.741	1236	.000
Only allows the transactions that are backed by a tangible asset.	.904	1236	.000
Does not approve financing of alcohol.	.909	1236	.000
Does not approve financing of pork.	.769	1236	.000
Does not approve financing of ammunitions	.827	1236	.000

Tobacco/Alcohol products	.806	1236	.000
All non-vegetarian Products	.851	1236	.000
Arms and Ammunition	.783	1236	.000
Non-Environment Friendly Products	.892	1236	.000
Products that involves animal cruelty	.772	1236	.000
a. Lilliefors Significance Correction			

Interpretation: The test statistics indicate the use of the Shapiro-Wilk test, specifically chosen for datasets smaller than 2000 elements. Given the dataset's size of 1236 elements, the Shapiro-Wilk test was applied. The obtained p-value is significant, leading to the acceptance of the alternative hypothesis, suggesting that the data is derived from a non-normal distribution. Consequently, it is imperative to employ non-parametric tests for subsequent statistical analyses.

3.12.2 Normalcy Analysis: Bank Officials' Data

Table 3.12- Tests of Normality: Bank Officials

Normality Test			
	Shapiro-Wilk		
	Statistic	df	Sig.
I am aware of the concept of **IFB** system.	.906	436	.000
The concept of **IFB** system can be implemented in India.	.906	436	.000
I am aware that **IFB** will not allow pre- determined fix amount of returns.	.894	436	.000
I am aware that in **IFB** profits will be allowed through trading activity only.	.892	436	.000
I am aware that in **IFB**, risk of loss and variability of profits will be faced by stakeholders to get the returns (profit and loss sharing).	.900	436	.000
I am aware that **IFB** will not consider time value of money with respect earning profit in form of interest.	.899	436	.000
I am aware that IFBS will not deal in the products that involve interest.	.891	436	.000

I am aware that **IFB** will be like a Partnership or joint venture.	.901	436	.000
I am aware that **IFB** will provide Sales contract.	.897	436	.000
I am aware that **IFB** will provide Leasing contract.	.888	436	.000
I am aware that **IFB** will provide Interest-free loans.	.891	436	.000
I am aware that **IFB** will provide special type of trading agreement.	.897	436	.000
Participation and equity principles are preserved.	.901	436	.000
There is Elimination of contract ambiguity and involvement of only real economic transactions having a tangible asset.	.866	436	.000
Economic activities that are morally and socially harmful are prohibited.	.858	436	.000
There is profit and loss sharing.	.895	436	.000
There is no investment of funds in the production of- Ammunitions, Alcohol and tobacco, Offensive advertising, Cruelty to animals.	.879	436	.000
There is no fixed rate of return on deposits nor is any interest charged on loans.	.892	436	.000
There is freedom from all forms of exploitations and there is justice between the financer and the entrepreneur.	.877	436	.000
Risk of loss and variability of profits must be faced to get the returns (profit and loss sharing)	.883	436	.000
IFB System has the business potential in India.	.901	436	.000
The customer base is large enough to start an alternative banking system.	.910	436	.000
With time, customer base of **IFB** can be increased.	.902	436	.000
IFSB should have transparency for business investments.	.880	436	.000
IFBS will be able to fulfill needs of depositors, investors and borrowers.	.917	436	.000
IFBS will be a good substitute for informal money	.879	436	.000

lending institutions.			
IFSB will be able to get enough investment.	.915	436	.000
IFBS will be able to gain enough profit.	.910	436	.000
IFBS needs to be governed by any specific regulatory body.	.874	436	.000
IFB System can be developed in India for all.	.896	436	.000
Potential to provide loans to those who do not have securities at disposal.	.881	436	.000
Potential to create value for each of the contracting parties involved	.914	436	.000
Potential to complement the existing Indian banking and finance system	.897	436	.000
Potential to contribute towards greater financial inclusion	.897	436	.000
Potential to support micro and small enterprises.	.892	436	.000
Potential to attract consumers from Arab countries.	.854	436	.000
Potential to benefit depositors as well as the bank.	.910	436	.000
Works on the principle of Prohibition of excessive risk/ uncertainty.	.892	436	.000
allows only the transactions that are backed by a tangible asset.	.905	436	.000
Does not approve financing of alcohol.	.908	436	.000
Does not approve financing of certain or all meat products.	.868	436	.000
Does not approve financing of ammunitions.	.898	436	.000
a. Lilliefors Significance Correction			

Interpretation: The test statistics reveal the application of the Shapiro-Wilk test, chosen for datasets with fewer than 2000 elements. Given the dataset's size of only 436 elements, the Shapiro-Wilk test was appropriately employed. The obtained p-value is significant, leading to the acceptance of the alternative hypothesis and a conclusive inference that the data originates from a non-normal distribution. Consequently, it is imperative to employ non-parametric tests for any subsequent statistical analyses.

3.13 Statistical Tools Used

- **Reliability Data Analysis**

According to Hair, Andersson, Tatham, Black & William, 1998, "the purpose of the reliability analysis is to determine whether data are trust worthy or not. Furthermore, Hair et al (1998) suggest that a series of diagnostic measures are to be used to assess internal consistency. Inter-item correlation (correlation should exceed 0.30), which measure correlation among items. Reliability investigation through Cronbach's Alpha is a method that is frequently used for assessing the consistency of entire scale. Due to its heavy usage, it is generally agreed that Cronbach's Alpha should exceed 0.60 to have reliability".

- **Normalcy Analysis**

According to Zahediasl S. & Ghasemi A. (2012), "assessing the normality assumption should be taken into account for using parametric statistical tests. It seems that the most popular test for normality, that is, the K-S test, should no longer be used owing to its low power. It is preferable that normality be assessed both visually and through normality tests, of which the Shapiro-Wilk test, provided by the SPSS software, is highly recommended. The normality assumption also needs to be considered for validation of data presented in the literature as it shows whether correct statistical tests have been used".

- **Factor Analysis**

"Factor analysis refers to the cluster of interdependence techniques where it summarizes the information from a large number of variables into factors, depending upon their relationships The purpose of factor analysis is to simplify the understanding of the data, which can be achieved from either an exploratory or confirmatory perspective (Hair et al, 1998). Factor Analysis is primarily an exploratory technique because of researcher's limited control over which variables are indicators of which latent construct. The scales usually start with many questions, and then by using factor analysis are reduced to a smaller number" (Pallant, 2007).

The condensed outcomes are subsequently employed in additional analyses, such as multiple regression analysis. For this study, exploratory factor analysis is utilized to pinpoint the pivotal factors associated with Awareness, Acceptability, Business Potential of **IFB**, and Religious considerations for General Public.

- **Chi-Square (c²) Analysis**

The chi-square (χ^2) tests are nonparametric and distribution-free, implying that no assumptions are required regarding the form of the original population distribution from which the samples are drawn. This characteristic makes the chi-square test significant among the various tests of significance developed by statisticians. In this study, Chi-square test was used to study the difference regarding Awareness Level, Acceptability level & Business Potential of **IFB** between Government Bank and Private Bank. The test was also applied to study the difference regarding Investing Behavior of respondents between their religions and difference regarding Awareness Level, Acceptability Level and Business Potential between respondent's demographic factors.

- **Regression Analysis**

"Regression analysis is used to find the relationship between one dependent variable and one or more independent variables and has become popular in many research areas" (Hair et al., 1998; Tabachnick & Fidell, 2007). "Regression analysis is called simple regression analysis when there is only one independent variable and is called multiple regression when there is more than one independent variable" (Robson, McGuire, 1999). "Multiple regression analysis is more complex than correlation and is used to find the ability of a set of independent variables in predicting the dependent variable" (Pallant, 2007). "The R square ranges from 0-1 and this shows how much of the dependent variable is explained by the independent variables. The higher the R square the stronger the association between the dependent variable and the independent variable" (Burns & Bush, 2010). In this study the researcher performed regression analysis to study the impact of Awareness Level (independent variable) on the Acceptability Level (dependent variable) from the perspective of General Public & Bank Officials. In addition the impact of Awareness Level & Acceptability Level (independent variables) on the Business Potential (dependent variable) from the perspective of General Public & Bank Officials was also studied.

- **Other Statistical Tests**

For the analysis of demographic factors and other banking services related factors, Frequency Analysis and Cross Tabulation Analysis were performed in the study.

- **Statistical Tools**

The researcher utilized the Statistical Package for Social Sciences (SPSS) and Microsoft Excel software to conduct the aforementioned statistical tests.

3.14 Ethical Issues

"In accordance with Wisker's principles outlined in 2008, adherence to ethical guidelines is imperative for researchers, particularly when human subjects are involved in the study. These ethical guidelines play a crucial role in protecting respondents from potential harm arising from their responses during interviews or any other research methodologies (De Leeuw, Hox & Dillman, 2008)".

To ensure the well-being of participants, confidentiality was diligently maintained. Respondents were explicitly informed that they had the option to include their names or provide any remarks that might reveal their identity. The researcher took comprehensive measures to address all facets of ethical considerations throughout the course of this research, thus upholding the highest ethical standards.

CHAPTER 4: DATA ANALYSIS AND INTERPRETATION

4.1 Introduction

The present chapter concerns with the presentation, analysis and interpretation of the data. In the present study, the researcher took **1672** respondents (**1236 respondents were General Public and 436 respondents were Bank Officials**. The following tools were administered for the purpose of collecting data-

1. **Awareness Level (of IFB) Scale** prepared by the researcher.
2. **Acceptability Level (of IFB) Scale** prepared by the researcher.
3. **Business Potential (of IFB) Scale** prepared by the researcher.

In this study, the data has been meticulously analyzed through textual discussions and presented in tables. The textual discussions served to highlight generalizations and provide significant interpretations, while the tables aimed to elucidate notable relationships. The construction of the tables ensured they are self-explanatory. To bring the study to a successful conclusion, the total data collected from **1672** respondents (**1236 from the General Public and 436 from Bank Officials**) regarding **"Business Potential of Interest Free Banking in India: A Study with Special Reference to Uttar Pradesh"** is being systematically organized, analyzed, and interpreted.

The raw data was initially organized into separate tables for each variable of the study. For the computation of necessary statistics and the application of appropriate statistical tests, most of the data was analyzed using Excel sheets and SPSS software. The analysis of the present study is detailed as follows -

4.2 Demographic Profile of the Respondents

Frequency analysis was found to be the most appropriate statistical test to analyse the respondents' demographic profile. There were two sets of respondents in this study-They were the General Public & the Bank Officials. The demographic analysis for each of them is presented separately in the sub-sections 4.2.1 & 4.2.2.

4.2.1 Demographic Profile of General Public

Table 4.1- City

City	Frequency	Percent	Cumulative Percent
Kanpur	144	11.7	11.7
Prayagraj	195	15.8	27.4
Lucknow	513	41.5	68.9
Azamgarh	231	18.7	87.6
Mau	153	12.4	100.0
Total	**1236**	**100.0**	

The table above illustrates that, among the total of 1236 respondents, 11.7% respondents were from Kanpur, 15.8% respondents were from Prayagraj, 41.5% respondents were from Lucknow, 18.7% respondents were from Azamgarh and 12.4% respondents were from Mau.

Table 4.2- Age

Age	Frequency	Percent	Cumulative Percent
21 years to 30	154	12.5	12.5
31 years to 40	618	50.0	62.5
41 years to 50	464	37.5	100.0
Total	**1236**	**100.0**	

The table above illustrates that, among the total of 1236 respondents, 12.5% respondents of age group 21-30 years, 50.0% respondents of age group 31-40 years and 37.5% respondents of age group 41-50 years.

Table 4.3- Gender

Gender	Frequency	Percent	Cumulative Percent
Male	816	66.0	66.0
Female	420	34.0	100.0
Total	**1236**	**100.0**	

The table above illustrates that, among the total of 1236 respondents, 66.0% respondents were male and 34.0% respondents were female.

Table 4.4- Religion

Religion	Frequency	Percent	Cumulative Percent
Hindu	604	48.9	48.9
Muslim	511	41.3	90.2
Christian	42	3.4	93.6
Sikh	28	2.3	95.9
Other	51	4.1	100.0
Total	**1236**	**100.0**	

The table above illustrates that, among the total of 1236 respondents, 48.9% respondents were Hindu, 41.3% respondents were Muslim, 3.4% respondents were Christian, 2.3% respondents were Sikh and 4.1% respondents were from other religions.

Table 4.5- Marital Status

Marital Status	Frequency	Percent	Cumulative Percent
Single	287	23.2	23.2
Married	918	74.3	97.5
Others	31	2.5	100.0
Total	**1236**	**100.0**	

The table above illustrates that, among the total of 1236 respondents, 23.2% respondents were single, 74.3% respondents were married and 2.5% respondents were others.

Table 4.6- Educational Qualifications

Educational Qualifications	Frequency	Percent	Cumulative Percent
Graduation	346	28.0	28.0
Post-Graduation	473	38.3	66.3
Professionally Qualified	120	9.7	76.0
Others	287	23.2	99.2
PhD	10	.8	100.0
Total	**1236**	**100.0**	

The table above illustrates that, among the total of 1236 respondents, 28.0% respondents were graduate, 38.3% respondents were post graduate, 9.7% respondents were professionally qualified, 23.2% respondents were others and 0.8% respondents were PhD.

Table 4.7- Occupation

Occupation	Frequency	Percent	Cumulative Percent
Private Job	382	30.9	30.9
Government Job	244	19.7	50.6
Business	553	44.7	95.4
Others	57	4.6	100.0
Total	**1236**	**100.0**	

The table above illustrates that, among the total of 1236 respondents, 30.9% respondents have private job, 19.7% respondents have government job, 44.7% respondents have businesses and 4.6% respondents were others

Table 4.8- Monthly Income

Monthly Income	Frequency	Percent	Cumulative Percent
Below Rs. 25,000	150	12.1	12.1
Between Rs. 25,001 to Rs. 50,000	323	26.1	38.3
Between Rs. 50,001 to Rs. 75,000	212	17.2	55.4
Between Rs. 75,001 to Rs. 1,00,000	439	35.5	90.9
Above Rs. 1,00,000	112	9.1	100.0
Total	**1236**	**100.0**	

The table above illustrates that, among the total of 1236 respondents, 12.1% respondent's monthly income was less than Rs. 25,000, 26.1% respondent's monthly income was between Rs. 25,001 – 50,000, 17.2% respondent's monthly income was between Rs. 50,001 – 75,000, 35.5% respondent's monthly income was between Rs. 75,001 – 1,00,000 and 9.1% respondent's monthly income was more than Rs. 1,00,000.

Table 4.9- Major Banking Services Availed

Major Banking Service	Frequency	Percent	Cumulative Percent
Savings a/c	742	60.0	60.0
Current a/c	251	20.3	80.3
Fixed Deposit	150	12.1	92.5
Mutual Funds	47	3.8	96.3
Other Investments Schemes	46	3.7	100.0
Total	**1236**	**100.0**	

The table above illustrates that, among the total of 1236 respondents, 60.0% respondents have savings account, 20.3% respondents have current account, 12.1% respondents have fixed deposits, 3.8% respondents have mutual funds and 3.7% respondents have other investments schemes.

Table 4.10- Major Purpose of Availing Banking Services

Purpose of Availing Banking	Frequency	Percent	Cumulative Percent
Secured Savings	1157	93.6	93.6
Investment involving risk	79	6.4	100.0
Total	1236	100.0	

The table above illustrates that, among the total of 1236 respondents, 93.6% respondents were availing banking services for secured savings and the rest 6.4% respondents were availing banking services for Investment involving risk.

Table 4.11- Investment Preference

Investment Preference	Frequency	Percent	Cumulative Percent
Low risk and low returns	1159	93.8	93.8
High risk and high returns	77	6.2	100.0
Total	1236	100.0	

The table above illustrates that, among the total of 1236 respondents, 93.8% respondents would prefer investments having low risk and low returns and 6.2% respondents would prefer investments having high risk and high returns.

4.2.2 Demographic Profile of Bank Officials

Table 4.12- City

City	Frequency	Percent	Cumulative Percent
Kanpur	44	10.1	10.1
Prayagraj	59	13.5	23.6
Lucknow	215	49.3	72.9
Azamgarh	70	16.1	89.0
Mau	48	11.0	100.0
Total	436	100.0	

The table above illustrates that, among the total of 436 respondents, 10.1% respondents were from Kanpur, 13.5% respondents were from Prayagraj, 49.3% respondents were from Lucknow, 16.1% respondents were from Azamgarh and 11.0% respondents were from Mau.

Table 4.13- Age

Age	Frequency	Percent	Cumulative Percent
21 years to 30 years	65	14.9	14.9
31 years to 40 years	182	41.7	56.7
41 years to 50 years	153	35.1	91.7
51 years to 60 years	36	8.3	100.0
Total	436	100.0	

The table above illustrates that, among the total of 436 respondents, 14.9% respondents of age group 21-30 years, 41.7% respondents of age group 31-40 years, 35.1% respondents of age group 41-50 years and 8.3% respondents of age group 51-60 years.

Table 4.14- Gender

Gender	Frequency	Percent	Cumulative Percent
Male	272	62.4	62.4
Female	164	37.6	100.0
Total	436	100.0	

The table above illustrates that, among the total of 436 respondents, 62.4% respondents were male and 37.6 respondents were female.

Table 4.15- Religion

Religion	Frequency	Percent	Cumulative Percent
Hindu	302	69.3	69.3
Islam	105	24.1	93.3
Sikh	14	3.2	96.6
Christian	15	3.4	100.0
Total	436	100.0	

The table above illustrates that, among the total of 436 respondents, 69.3% respondents were Hindu, 24.1% respondents were Muslim, 3.4% respondents were Christian and 3.2% respondents were Sikh.

Table 4.16- Marital Status

Marital Status	Frequency	Percent	Cumulative Percent
Single	123	28.2	28.2
Married	313	71.8	100.0
Total	436	100.0	

The table above illustrates that, among the total of 436 respondents, 28.2% respondents were single and 71.8% respondents were married.

Table 4.17- Educational Qualifications

Educational Qualifications	Frequency	Percent	Cumulative Percent
Graduation/Post-Graduation	117	26.8	26.8
Professionally/Technically Qualified	228	52.3	79.1
Others	91	20.9	100.0
Total	436	100.0	

The table above illustrates that, among the total of 436 respondents, 26.8% respondents were graduate, 52.3% respondents professionally/ technically qualified and 20.9% respondents were others.

Table 4.18- Designation

Designation	Frequency	Percent	Cumulative Percent
Lower Level Executive	159	36.5	36.5
Middle Level Executive	221	50.7	87.2
Higher Level Executive	56	12.8	100.0
Total	436	100.0	

The table above illustrates that, among the total of 436 respondents, 36.5% respondents were lower level executive, 50.7% respondents were middle level executive and 12.8% respondents were higher level executive.

Table 4.19- Type of Bank

Type of Bank	Frequency	Percent	Cumulative Percent
Government Bank	253	58.0	58.0
Private Bank	183	42.0	100.0
Total	**436**	**100.0**	

The table above illustrates that, among the total of 436 respondents, 58.0% respondents were from government bank and 42.0% respondents were from private bank.

Table 4.20- Distribution of Private and Government Banks City wise

Cities * Type of bank Cross Tabulation					
			Type of bank		
			Government Bank	Private Bank	Total
	Kanpur	Count	28	16	44
		% within	63.6%	36.4%	100.0%
	Prayagraj	Count	33	26	59
		% within	55.9%	44.1%	100.0%
Cities	Lucknow	Count	119	96	215
		% within	55.3%	44.7%	100.0%
	Azamgarh	Count	42	28	70
		% within	60.0%	40.0%	100.0%
	Mau	Count	31	17	48
		% within	64.6%	35.4%	100.0%
Total		Count	253	183	436
		% within	58.0%	42.0%	100.0%

From the above table, city wise distribution of bank officials from government bank and private bank can be seen, the details of which are given below-

- **Kanpur:** In case of Kanpur, there were total 44 respondents (bank officials) out of which 63.6% bank officials were from government bank and 36.4% bank officials were from private bank.

- **Prayagraj:** In case of Prayagraj, there were total 59 respondents (bank officials) out of which 55.9% bank officials were from government bank and 44.1% bank officials were from private bank.

- **Lucknow:** In case of Lucknow, there were total 215 respondents (bank officials) out of which 55.3% bank officials were from government bank and44.7% bank officials were from private bank.

- **Azamgarh:** In case of Azamgarh, there were total 70 respondents (bank officials) out of which 60.0% bank officials were from government bank and40.0% bank officials were from private bank.

- **Mau:** In case of Mau, there were total 48 respondents (bank officials) out of which 64.6% bank officials were from government bank and35.4% bank officials were from private bank.

4.3 Research Objective 1: To test the Awareness Level of Respondents regarding IFB.

4.3.1 Factor Analysis: Identifying the most important factors of Awareness of IFB for General Public.

Table 4.21- KMO and Bartlett's Test

KMO and Bartlett's Test		
Kaiser-Meyer-Olkin Measure of Sampling Adequacy.		**.739**
Bartlett's Test of Sphericity	Approx. Chi-Square	2223.539
	df	91
	Sig.	.000

The KMO measure of sampling adequacy is **0.739** which indicates the present data is suitable for factor analysis. Similarly, Bartlett's test of sphericity is significant (p < 0.001); that explains existence of sufficient correlation between variables to proceed with the analysis.

Table 4.22- Total Variance Explained

Component	Initial Eigen values			Extraction Sums of Squared Loadings			Rotation Sums of Squared Loadings		
	Total	% of Variance	Cumulative%	Total	% of Variance	Cumulative%	Total	% of Variance	Cumulative%
1	2.840	**20.286**	20.286	2.840	20.286	20.286	1.818	12.985	12.985
2	1.791	**12.793**	33.080	1.791	12.793	33.080	1.794	12.812	25.797
3	1.248	**8.917**	41.997	1.248	8.917	41.997	1.697	12.124	37.920
4	1.031	**7.363**	49.360	1.031	7.363	49.360	1.435	10.250	48.171
5	1.025	**7.322**	56.682	1.025	7.322	56.682	1.192	8.511	56.682
6	.871	6.225	62.906						
7	.836	5.970	68.876						
8	.763	5.450	74.326						
9	.716	5.113	79.439						
10	.656	4.686	84.125						
11	.629	4.492	88.618						
12	.581	4.150	92.768						
13	.519	3.709	96.476						
14	.493	3.524	100.000						
Extraction Method: Principal Component Analysis.									

Findings and Interpretation: The table above displays eight values corresponding to each linear component (factor) at different stages: before extraction, after extraction, and after rotation. Prior to extraction, Output identified **5** linear components within the dataset. Following extraction and rotation, the primary factor **(Factor 1) accounted for 20.286% of the total variance, Factor 2 explained 12.793%, Factor 3 explained 8.917%, Factor 4 explained 7.363%, and Factor 5 explained 7.322% of the total variance** that could be extracted. The table on Total Variations Explained reveals that among the 5 components, the first factor is deemed the most crucial and extractable, as evident from the percentages outlined.

Table 4.23- Rotated Component Matrix

Rotated Component Matrix[a]					
	Component				
	1	2	3	4	5
I am aware that **IFB** provides Interest-free loans.	**.773**	.007	-.080	.219	.051
I am aware that **IFB** provides Trade with markup.	**.705**	.067	.211	-.112	.081
I am aware that **IFB** provides special type of trading agreement.	**.617**	.071	.270	-.048	.091
I am aware that **IFB** does not allow pre-determined fix amount of returns.	.056	**.800**	.021	.001	.038
I am aware of the concept of **IFB** system.	.074	**.796**	.061	.032	.117
I am aware that in **IFB** profits are allowed through trading activity only.	.016	**.673**	.053	.236	-.015
I am aware that **IFB** has the system of Profit and loss sharing.	-.038	.054	**.737**	.017	.114
I am aware that **IFB** is a kind of Partnerships or joint ventures.	.161	.020	**.683**	.032	.120
I am aware that **IFB** provides Sales contract.	.346	.054	**.605**	.088	-.072
I am aware that **IFB** provides Leasing contract.	.391	.049	**.403**	.051	-.219
I am aware that in **IFB** risk of loss and variability of profits must be faced to get the returns (profit and loss sharing).	-.026	.144	.105	**.806**	-.007
I am aware that **IFB** does not believe in time value of money with respect earning profit in form of interest.	.078	.083	.008	**.791**	.187
I am aware that IFBS does not deal in the products that involve interest.	-.024	.139	-.002	.011	**.760**
I am aware that pre-determined fix amount	.161	-.018	.130	.167	**.683**

of returns is not allowed in IFBS					
Extraction Method: Principal Component Analysis.					
Rotation Method: Varimax with Kaiser Normalization.					
a. Rotation converged in 6 iterations.					

Findings: Most Important factors of Awareness of IFB for General Public.

In the current investigation, Factor Analysis showcases the rotated factor loadings associated with the statements (variables) representing the most significant factors related to the **Awareness of IFB** for the **General Public**.

From the above **Table 4.23-** of Rotated Component Matrix, it was found that-

Factor- 1 (IFB Services Awareness) includes following **3** variables

1. I am aware that **IFB** provides Interest-free loans.
2. I am aware that **IFB** provides Trade with mark-up.
3. I am aware that **IFB** provides special type of trading agreement.

Factor- 2 (IFB Operations Awareness) includes following **3** variables

1. I am aware that **IFB** does not allow pre-determined fix amount of returns.
2. I am aware of the concept of **IFB** system.
3. I am aware that in **IFB** profits are allowed through trading activity only.

Factor- 3 (IFB Financial Instruments Awareness) includes following **4** variables

1. I am aware that **IFB** has the system of Profit and loss sharing.
2. I am aware that **IFB** is a kind of partnerships or joint ventures.
3. I am aware that **IFB** provides Sales contract.
4. I am aware that **IFB** provides Leasing contract.

Factor- 4 (PLS Awareness) includes following **2** variables

1. I am aware that in **IFB** risk of loss and variability of profits must be faced to get the returns (profit and loss sharing).
2. I am aware that **IFB** does not believe in time value of money with respect earning profit in form of interest.

Factor- 5 (IFB Practices) includes following **2** variables

1. I am aware that IFBS does not deal in the products that involve interest.
2. I am aware that pre-determined fix amount of returns is not allowed in IFBS.

4.3.2 Factor Analysis: Identifying the most important factors of Awareness of IFB for Bank Officials.

Factor Analysis was conducted to identify the predominant factors influencing the **Awareness of IFB** among **Bank Officials**.

Table 4.24- KMO and Bartlett's Test

KMO and Bartlett's Test		
Kaiser-Meyer-Olkin Measure of Sampling Adequacy.		**.786**
Bartlett's Test of Sphericity	Approx. Chi-Square	970.391
	df	66
	Sig.	.000

The KMO measure of sampling adequacy is **0.786** which indicates the present data is suitable for factor analysis. Similarly, Bartlett's test of sphericity is significant ($p < 0.001$); that explains existence of sufficient correlation between variables to proceed with the analysis.

Table 4.25- Total Variance Explained

Total Variance Explained									
Component	Initial Eigenvalues			Extraction Sums of Squared Loadings			Rotation Sums of Squared Loadings		
	Total	% of Variance	Cumulative%	Total	% of Variance	Cumulative%	Total	% of Variance	Cumulative%
1	3.439	**28.655**	28.655	3.439	28.655	28.655	2.123	17.691	17.691
2	1.471	**12.259**	40.914	1.471	12.259	40.914	2.052	17.096	34.788
3	1.099	**9.161**	50.075	1.099	9.161	50.075	1.835	15.288	50.075
4	.925	7.708	57.784						
5	.873	7.274	65.058						
6	.779	6.495	71.553						
7	.733	6.112	77.665						
8	.664	5.533	83.197						
9	.581	4.841	88.039						
10	.559	4.654	92.693						

11	.490	4.087	96.780						
12	.386	3.220	100.000						
Extraction Method: Principal Component Analysis.									

Findings and Interpretation: In the table above, the output displays eight values corresponding to each linear component (factor) before extraction, after extraction, and after rotation. Initially, Output identified **3** linear components within the dataset before extraction. Following extraction and rotation, the primary factor **(Factor 1) accounted for 28.655% of the total variance, Factor 2 explained 12.259%, and Factor 3 explained 9.161%** of the total variance that could be extracted. As indicated in the Total Variations Explained table, it was observed that among the total 3 components, the first factor is the most significant and extractable.

Table 4.26- Rotated Component Matrix

Rotated Component Matrix[a]			
	Component		
	1	2	3
I am aware that **IFB** will provide Interest-free loans.	**.781**	.091	.079
I am aware that **IFB** will provide special type of trading agreement.	**.692**	.249	.069
I am aware that **IFB** will provide Leasing contract.	**.679**	.036	.060
I am aware that **IFB** will provide Sales contract.	**.473**	.056	.397
The concept of **IFB** system can be implemented in India.	.111	**.789**	.039
I am aware that **IFB** will not allow pre- determined fix amount of returns.	-.003	**.660**	.293
I am aware of the concept of **IFB** system.	.317	**.648**	-.055
I am aware that in **IFB** profits will be allowed through trading activity only.	.072	**.538**	.453
I am aware that **IFB** will not consider time value of money with respect earning profit in form of interest.	-.054	.081	**.657**
I am aware that **IFB** will be like a Partnership or joint venture.	.404	-.045	**.587**
I am aware that IFBS will not deal in the products that involve interest.	.255	.162	**.573**

I am aware that in **IFB**, risk of loss and variability of profits will be faced by stakeholders to get the returns (profit and loss sharing).	-.010	.419	**.511**
Extraction Method: Principal Component Analysis. Rotation Method: Varimax with Kaiser Normalization.			
a. Rotation converged in 7 iterations.			

Findings: Most Important factors of Awareness of IFB for Bank Officials.

In this current study, Factor Analysis reveals the rotated factor loadings for the statements (variables) representing the most crucial factors associated with the **Awareness of IFB among Bank Officials.**

Table- 4.26 of Rotated Component Matrix, showed that-

Factor- 1 (IFB Services Awareness) includes following **4** variables

1. I am aware that **IFB** will provide Interest-free loans.
2. I am aware that **IFB** will provide special type of trading agreement.
3. I am aware that **IFB** will provide Leasing contract.
4. I am aware that **IFB** will provide Sales contract.

Factor- 2 (IFB System Understanding) includes following **4** variables

1. The concept of **IFB** system can be implemented in India.
2. I am aware that **IFB** will not allow pre-determined fix amount of returns.
3. I am aware of the concept of **IFB** System.
4. I am aware that in **IFB** profits will be allowed through trading activity only.

Factor- 3 (IFB Principles Understanding) includes following **4** variables

1. I am aware that **IFB** will not consider time value of money with respect earning profit in form of interest.
2. I am aware that **IFB** will be like a Partnership or joint venture.
3. I am aware that IFBS will not deal in the products that involve interest.
4. I am aware that in **IFB**, risk of loss and variability of profits will be faced by stakeholders to get the returns (profit and loss sharing).

4.3.3 Chi Square Analysis: Difference between Male and Female Respondents among General Public regarding Awareness Level of IFB.

$H_{01.1}$: *There is no significant difference between Male and Female Respondents among General Public regarding Awareness Level of IFB.*

Table 4.27- Chi Square Tests: Gender wise Awareness Level (General Public)

Chi-Square Tests			
	Value	df	Asymp. Sig. (2-sided)
Pearson Chi-Square	18.401[a]	4	.001

Findings and Interpretation: As per the Chi Square Tests, Pearson Chi-Square comes out to be significant (p value .001<.05). It means that there is significant difference between Male and Female respondents among General Public regarding Awareness level of IFB. Therefore $H_{01.1}$ is rejected.

Table 4.28- Crosstab

Gender * Awareness Level Cross Tabulation								
			Awareness Level					
			Very Low Level	Low Level	Moderate Level	High Level	Very High Level	Total
Gender	Male	Count	35	169	331	241	40	816
		% within	4.3%	20.7%	40.6%	29.5%	4.9%	100.0%
	Female	Count	6	64	189	149	12	420
		% within	1.4%	15.2%	45.0%	35.5%	2.9%	100.0%
Total		Count	41	233	520	390	52	1236
		% within	3.3%	18.9%	42.1%	31.6%	4.2%	100.0%

Findings and Interpretation:

- **Male: Out of total 816 respondents,** 4.3% respondents have very low level, 20.7% respondents have low level, 40.6% respondents have moderate level, 29.5% respondents have high level and 4.9% respondents have very high Awareness Level.

- **Female: Out of total 420 respondents,** 1.4% respondents have very low level, 15.2% respondents have low level, 45.0% respondents have moderate level, 35.5% respondents have high level and 2.9% respondents have very high Awareness Level.

4.3.4 Chi Square Analysis: Difference between Government Bank and Private Bank Respondents among Bank Officials regarding Awareness Level of IFB.

H_{01-2}: *There is no significant difference between Government Bank and Private Bank Respondents among Bank Officials regarding Awareness Level of IFB.*

Table 4.29- Chi Square Tests: Bank wise Awareness Level

Chi-Square Tests			
	Value	df	Asymptotic Significance (2-sided)
Pearson Chi-Square	2.485[a]	4	.647

Findings and Interpretation: As per the Chi Square Tests, Pearson Chi-Square comes out to be insignificant (p value .647<.05). It means there is no significant difference regarding Awareness Level of IFB among Bank Officials between Government Bank and Private Bank respondents. Therefore H_{01-2} is accepted.

4.4 Research Objective 2: To identify whether current Banks (Private as well as Govt.) will be ready to introduce IFB or not if investors are ready to adopt it.

4.4.1 Factor Analysis: Identifying the most important factors of Acceptability about IFB for General Public.

Table 4.30- KMO and Bartlett's Test

KMO and Bartlett's Test		
Kaiser-Meyer-Olkin Measure of Sampling Adequacy.		.710
Bartlett's Test of Sphericity	Approx. Chi-Square	3475.975
	df	36
	Sig.	.000

The KMO measure of sampling adequacy is **0.710** which indicates the present data is suitable for factor analysis. Similarly, Bartlett's test of sphericity is significant (p < 0.001); that explains existence of sufficient correlation between variables to proceed with the analysis.

Table 4.31- Total Variance Explained

Component	Initial Eigenvalues			Extraction Sums of Squared Loadings			Rotation Sums of Squared Loadings		
	Total	% of Variance	Cumulative%	Total	% of Variance	Cumulative%	Total	% of Variance	Cumulative%
1	3.053	**33.918**	33.918	3.053	33.918	33.918	2.323	25.815	25.815
2	1.580	**17.552**	51.470	1.580	17.552	51.470	2.150	23.890	49.705
3	1.022	**11.357**	62.827	1.022	11.357	62.827	1.181	13.122	62.827
4	.991	11.006	73.833						
5	.933	10.364	84.197						
6	.479	5.321	89.518						
7	.452	5.023	94.542						
8	.254	2.826	97.368						
9	.237	2.632	100.000						

Extraction Method: Principal Component Analysis.

Findings and Interpretation: In the table above, the output displays eight values associated with each linear component (factor) before extraction, after extraction, and after rotation. Initially, Output identified **3** linear components within the dataset before extraction. Following extraction and rotation, the primary **factor (Factor 1) explained 33.918% of the total variance, Factor 2 explained 17.552%, and Factor 3 explained 11.357%** of the total variance that could be extracted. The Total Variations Explained table indicates that among the 3 components, the first factor is the most significant and can be extracted.

Table 4.32- Rotated Component Matrix

Rotated Component Matrix[a]	Component		
	1	2	3
There is Elimination of contract ambiguity and involvement of only real economic transactions having a tangible asset.	.886	.163	.068
Economic activities that are morally and socially harmful are prohibited.	.868	.111	.038
Participation and equity principles are preserved.	.798	.145	.101

There is profit and loss sharing.	**-.164**	.094	.034
There is freedom from all forms of exploitations and there is justice between the financer and the entrepreneur	.032	**.800**	-.102
Increase in return produced by trading is welcomed but by interest is prohibited.	-.018	**.792**	-.098
There is no investment of funds in the production of-Ammunitions, Alcohol and tobacco, Offensive advertising, Cruelty to animals.	.198	**.665**	.490
There is no fixed rate of return on deposits nor is any interest charged on loans.	.280	**.597**	.491
Risk of loss and variability of profits must be faced to get the returns (profit and loss sharing)	.043	.119	**-.814**
Extraction Method: Principal Component Analysis. Rotation Method: Varimax with Kaiser Normalization.			
a. Rotation converged in 4 iterations.			

Findings: Most Important factors of Acceptability about IFB for General Public.

In the current study, Factor Analysis presents the rotated factor loadings for the statements (variables) representing the most crucial factors related to the **Acceptability of IFB for the General Public.**

Looking at table of Rotated Component Matrix, it was found that-

Factor- 1 (Principles of Participation and Equity Preservation) includes following **4** variables

1. There is Elimination of contract ambiguity and involvement of only real economic transactions having a tangible asset.
2. Economic activities that are morally and socially harmful are prohibited.
3. Participation and equity principles are preserved.
4. There is profit and loss sharing.

Factor- 2 (Justice in Financer-Entrepreneur Relationships) includes following **4** variables

1. There is freedom from all forms of exploitations and there is justice between the financer and the entrepreneur.

2. Increase in return produced by trading is welcomed but by interest is prohibited.

3. There is no investment of funds in the production of- Ammunitions, Alcohol and tobacco, Offensive advertising, Cruelty to animals.

4. There is no fixed rate of return on deposits nor is any interest charged on loans.

Factor- 3 (PLS Principle) includes following **1** variable

1. Risk of loss and variability of profits must be faced to get the returns (profit and loss sharing)

4.4.2 Factor Analysis: Identifying the most important factors of Acceptability about IFB for Bank Officials.

Factor Analysis was performed to determine the most important factors of **Acceptability about IFB for Bank Officials.**

Table 4.33- KMO and Bartlett's Test

KMO and Bartlett's Test		
Kaiser-Meyer-Olkin Measure of Sampling Adequacy.		**.622**
Bartlett's Test of Sphericity	Approx. Chi-Square	661.662
	Df	28
	Sig.	.000

The KMO measure of sampling adequacy is **0.622** which indicates the present data is suitable for factor analysis. Similarly, Bartlett's test of sphericity is significant (p < 0.001); that explains existence of sufficient correlation between variables to proceed with the analysis.

Table 4.34-Total Variance Explained

Total Variance Explained								
Component	Initial Eigenvalues			Extraction Sums of Squared Loadings			Rotation Sums of Squared Loadings		
	Total	% of Variance	Cumulative%	Total	% of Variance	Cumulative%	Total	% of Variance	Cumulative%
1	2.456	**30.697**	30.697	2.456	30.697	30.697	2.013	25.160	25.160
2	1.568	**19.599**	50.297	1.568	19.599	50.297	1.614	20.170	45.330
3	1.054	**13.173**	63.470	1.054	13.173	63.470	1.451	18.140	63.470
4	.766	9.575	73.045						
5	.684	8.551	81.597						
6	.616	7.698	89.294						

7	.565	7.057	96.351						
8	.292	3.649	100.000						
Extraction Method: Principal Component Analysis.									

Findings and Interpretation: In the table above, the output lists eight values associated with each linear component (factor) before extraction, after extraction, and after rotation. Prior to extraction, Output identified **3** linear components within the dataset. Following extraction and rotation, the primary factor **(Factor 1) explained 30.697% of the total variance, Factor 2 explained 19.599%, and Factor 3 explained 13.173%** of the total variance that could be extracted. The Total Variations Explained table indicates that among the 3 components, the first factor is the most crucial and can be extracted.

Table 4.35- Rotated Component Matrix

Rotated Component Matrix[a]			
	Component		
	1	2	3
There is freedom from all forms of exploitations and there is justice between the financer and the entrepreneur.	**.891**	.051	.067
Risk of loss and variability of profits must be faced to get the returns (profit and loss sharing)	**.755**	.002	.112
There is no fixed rate of return on deposits nor is any interest charged on loans.	**.737**	.025	.199
Participation and equity principles are preserved.	.175	**.807**	-.213
Economic activities that are morally and socially harmful are prohibited.	-.020	**.709**	.215
There is Elimination of contract ambiguity and involvement of only real economic transactions having a tangible asset.	-.067	**.656**	.331
There is profit and loss sharing.	.121	.080	**.844**
There is no investment of funds in the production of- Ammunitions, Alcohol and tobacco, Offensive advertising, Cruelty to animals.	.238	.142	**.694**
Extraction Method: Principal Component Analysis. Rotation Method: Varimax with Kaiser Normalization.			
a. Rotation converged in 5 iterations.			

Findings: Most Important factors of Acceptability about IFB for Bank Officials.

In this current study, Factor Analysis displays the rotated factor loadings for the statements (variables) representing the most significant factors associated with the **Acceptability of IFB among Bank Officials.**

Looking at table of Rotated Component Matrix, it was found that-

Factor- 1 (Financial Justice in IFB) includes following **3** variables
1. There is freedom from all forms of exploitations and there is justice between the financer and the entrepreneur.
2. Risk of loss and variability of profits must be faced to get the returns (profit and loss sharing)
3. There is no fixed rate of return on deposits nor is any interest charged on loans.

Factor- 2 (Preservation of Participation and Equity) includes following **3** variables
1. Participation and equity principles are preserved.
2. Economic activities that are morally and socially harmful are prohibited.
3. There is Elimination of contract ambiguity and involvement of only real economic transactions having a tangible asset.

Factor- 3 (PLS Principle) includes following **2** variables
1. There is profit and loss sharing.
2. There is no investment of funds in the production of- Ammunitions, Alcohol and tobacco, Offensive advertising, Cruelty to animals.

4.4.3 Regression Analysis: Impact of Awareness Level on Acceptability Level from the perspective of General Public.

$H_{02.1}$: There is no significant impact of Awareness Level on the Acceptability Level of IFB from the perspective of General Public.

Table 4.36- ANOVA: Impact of Awareness on Acceptability (General Public)

ANOVA[a]						
Model		Sum of Squares	Df	Mean Square	F	Sig.
1	Regression	2.089	1	2.089	2.911	.088[b]
	Residual	885.532	1234	.718		
	Total	887.621	1235			
a. Dependent Variable: Acceptability Level						
b. Predictors: (Constant), Awareness Level						

94

Findings and Interpretation: The p-value (0.088) associated with F value came out be more than 0.05. It means there is no significant impact of Awareness Level on the Acceptability Level and independent variable (IV) of our study does not **reliably predict** the dependent variable (DV).

4.4.4 Regression Analysis: Impact of Awareness Level on Acceptability Level from the perspective of Bank Officials.

$H_{02.2}$: There is no significant impact of Awareness Level on the Acceptability Level of IFB from the perspective of Bank Officials.

Table 4.37- ANOVA: Impact of Awareness on Acceptability (Bank Officials)

ANOVA[a]						
Model		Sum of Squares	df	Mean Square	F	Sig.
1	Regression	5.707	1	5.707	4.753	.030[b]
	Residual	521.045	434	1.201		
	Total	526.752	435			
a. Dependent Variable: Acceptability Level						
b. Predictors: (Constant), Awareness Level						

Findings and Interpretation: The p-value (0.030) associated with F value came out be less than 0.05. It means there is significant impact of Awareness Level on the Acceptability Level and independent variable (IV) of our study **reliably predicts** the dependent variable (DV).

Table 4.38- Model Summary

Model Summary				
Model	R	R Square	Adjusted R Square	Std. Error of the Estimate
1	.104[a]	.011	.009	1.096
a. Predictors: (Constant), Awareness Level				

The analysis explored that the value of R square with the help of model summary table as given by the output. From the Model summary it was found that the proportion of explained variance as measured by R-Square was **(R2=0.011)** that signifies of about **01.1%** of the variance in **Acceptability Level** (dependent Variable) was explained by **Awareness Level** (independent variable).

Table 4.39- Coefficient

	Model	Unstandardized Coefficients		Standardized Coefficients	t	Sig.
		B	Std. Error	Beta		
1	(Constant)	2.818	.172		16.414	.000
	Awareness Level	.126	.058	.104	2.18	.030
a. Dependent Variable: Acceptability Level						

Findings: Awareness Level: From the above table it was found the value of unstandardized-coefficients (Beta) is **0.126;** which is a positive value signifying that a 1-unit positive standard deviation change in it would bring **increase** in the standard deviation of dependent variable **Acceptability Level** by **0.126** unit.

Thus, on the ground that the value of coefficient is significant at **.030** level, $H_{02.2}$ is rejected and concluded that Awareness Level have significant and positive impact on Acceptability Level in case of Bank Official's perspective.

4.4.5 Chi-Square Analysis: Difference between Male and Female Respondents among General Public regarding Acceptability of IFB.

$H_{02.3}$: *There is no significant difference between Male and Female Respondents among General Public regarding Acceptability Level of IFB.*

Table 4.40- Chi Square Tests: Gender wise Acceptability Level (General Public)

Chi-Square Tests			
	Value	df	Asymp. Sig. (2-sided)
Pearson Chi-Square	19.106[a]	4	.001

Findings and Interpretation: As per the Chi Square Tests, Pearson Chi-Square comes out to be insignificant (p value 0.001<.05). It means that there is significant difference between Male and Female respondents among General Public regarding Acceptability of IFB. Therefore $H_{02.3}$ is rejected.

Table 4.41- Crosstab

<table>
<tr><td colspan="9" align="center">Gender * Acceptability Level Cross Tabulation</td></tr>
<tr><td rowspan="2"></td><td rowspan="2"></td><td rowspan="2"></td><td colspan="5" align="center">Acceptability Level</td><td rowspan="2">Total</td></tr>
<tr><td>Very Low Level</td><td>Low Level</td><td>Moderate Level</td><td>High Level</td><td>Very High Level</td></tr>
<tr><td rowspan="4">Gender</td><td rowspan="2">Male</td><td>Count</td><td>16</td><td>110</td><td>320</td><td>321</td><td>49</td><td>816</td></tr>
<tr><td>% within</td><td>2.0%</td><td>13.5%</td><td>39.2%</td><td>39.3%</td><td>6.0%</td><td>100.0%</td></tr>
<tr><td rowspan="2">Female</td><td>Count</td><td>10</td><td>55</td><td>214</td><td>118</td><td>23</td><td>420</td></tr>
<tr><td>% within</td><td>2.4%</td><td>13.1%</td><td>51.0%</td><td>28.1%</td><td>5.5%</td><td>100.0%</td></tr>
<tr><td colspan="2" rowspan="2">Total</td><td>Count</td><td>26</td><td>165</td><td>534</td><td>439</td><td>72</td><td>1236</td></tr>
<tr><td>% within</td><td>2.1%</td><td>13.3%</td><td>43.2%</td><td>35.5%</td><td>5.8%</td><td>100.0%</td></tr>
</table>

Findings and Interpretation:

- **Male: Out of total 816 respondents,** 2.0% respondents have very low level, 13.5% respondents have low level, 39.2% respondents have moderate level, 39.3% respondents have high level and 6.0% respondents have very high Acceptability Level.

- **Female: Out of total 420 respondents,** 2.4% respondents have very low level, 13.1% respondents have low level, 51.0% respondents have moderate level, 28.1% respondents have high level and 5.5% respondents have very high Acceptability Level.

4.4.6 Chi-Square Analysis: Difference between Government Bank and Private Bank Respondents among Bank Officials regarding Acceptability Level of IFB.

$H_{02.4}$: *There is no significant difference between Government Bank and Private Bank Respondents among Bank Officials regarding Acceptability Level of IFB.*

Table 4.42- Chi Square Tests: Bank wise Acceptability Level

<table>
<tr><td colspan="4" align="center">Chi-Square Tests</td></tr>
<tr><td></td><td>Value</td><td>df</td><td>Asymptotic Significance (2-sided)</td></tr>
<tr><td>Pearson Chi-Square</td><td>6.120[a]</td><td>4</td><td>.190</td></tr>
</table>

Findings and Interpretation: As per the Chi Square Tests, Pearson Chi-Square comes out to be insignificant (p value .190<.05). It means that there is no significant difference between Government Bank and Private Bank respondents regarding Acceptability Level of IFB. Therefore $H_{02.4}$ is accepted.

4.5 Research Objective 3: To explore the Business Potential of IFB in India.

4.5.1 Factor Analysis: Identifying the most important factors of Business Potential of IFB and Religious aspects for General Public.

Factor Analysis was performed to determine the most important factors of **Business Potential of IFB and Religious Aspects for General Public.**

Table 4.43- KMO and Bartlett's Test

KMO and Bartlett's Test		
Kaiser-Meyer-Olkin Measure of Sampling Adequacy.		.787
Bartlett's Test of Sphericity	Approx. Chi-Square	14388.613
	Df	78
	Sig.	.000

The KMO measure of sampling adequacy is **0.787** which indicates the present data is suitable for factor analysis. Similarly, Bartlett's test of sphericity is significant (p < 0.001); that explains existence of sufficient correlation between variables to proceed with the analysis.

Table 4.44- Total Variance Explained

Total Variance Explained									
Compo nent	Initial Eigenvalues			Extraction Sums of Squared Loadings			Rotation Sums of Squared Loadings		
	Total	% of Variance	Cumulative%	Total	% of Variance	Cumulative%	Total	% of Variance	Cumulative%
1	5.973	**45.949**	45.949	5.973	45.949	45.949	3.474	26.726	26.726
2	2.230	**17.156**	63.105	2.230	17.156	63.105	2.609	20.072	46.799
3	1.360	**10.461**	73.567	1.360	10.461	73.567	2.421	18.626	65.425
4	1.098	**8.446**	82.013	1.098	8.446	82.013	2.156	16.588	82.013
5	.595	4.573	86.586						
6	.414	3.182	89.769						
7	.400	3.080	92.849						
8	.296	2.281	95.129						
9	.242	1.860	96.989						

10	.155	1.196	98.185						
11	.125	.961	99.145						
12	.062	.477	99.622						
13	.049	.378	100.000						
Extraction Method: Principal Component Analysis.									

Findings and Interpretation: In the table above, the output lists eight values associated with each linear component (factor) before extraction, after extraction, and after rotation. Prior to extraction, Output identified **4** linear components within the dataset. Following extraction and rotation, the primary factor **(Factor 1) explained 45.949% of the total variance, Factor 2 explained 17.156%, Factor 3 explained 10.461%, and Factor 4 explained 8.446%** of the total variance that could be extracted. The Total Variations Explained table indicates that among the 4 components, the first factor is the most crucial and can be extracted.

Table 4.45- Rotated Component Matrix

Rotated Component Matrix[a]				
	Component			
	1	2	3	4
Only allows the transactions that are backed by a tangible asset.	**.842**	.128	.253	.132
Emphasizes social activities	**.829**	.075	.266	.182
That works on the principle of Prohibition of excessive risk/ uncertainty.	**.722**	.215	.058	.302
Potential to benefit depositors as well as the bank.	**.615**	-.034	-.025	.587
Does not approve financing of pork.	-.012	**.955**	.041	.052
Does not approve financing of alcohol.	.260	**.893**	.203	.054
Does not approve financing of ammunitions	.096	**.849**	.120	.090
Potential to provide loans to those who do not have securities at disposal.	.286	.060	**.833**	.160
Potential to create value for each of the contracting parties involved	.334	.057	**.827**	.216
Potential to complement the existing Indian banking and finance system	.050	.270	**.781**	.159
Potential to contribute towards greater financial inclusion	.236	.101	.275	**.887**

Potential to support micro and small enterprises.	.263	.132	.305	**.868**

Extraction Method: Principal Component Analysis.

Rotation Method: Varimax with Kaiser Normalization.

a. Rotation converged in 5 iterations.

Findings: Most Important factors of Business Potential of IFB and Religious Aspects for General Public.

In this present study, Factor Analysis presents the rotated factor loadings for the statements (variables) related to the most prominent factors concerning the **Business Potential of IFB and Religious Aspects for the general public.**

Looking at table of Rotated Component Matrix, it was found that-

Factor- 1 (Emphasis on Social Justice) includes following **4** variables

1. Only allows the transactions that are backed by a tangible asset.
2. Emphasizes social activities.
3. That works on the principle of prohibition of excessive risk/ uncertainty.
4. Potential to benefit depositors as well as the bank.

Factor- 2 (Emphasis on Ethical Values) includes following **3** variables

1. Does not approve financing of pork.
2. Does not approve financing of alcohol.
3. Does not approve financing of ammunitions.

Factor- 3 (Financial Alternative) includes following **3** variables

1. Potential to provide loans to those who do not have securities at disposal.
2. Potential to create value for each of the contracting parties involved.
3. Potential to complement the existing Indian banking and finance system.

Factor- 4 (Greater Financial Inclusion) includes following **2** variables

1. Potential to contribute towards greater financial inclusion.
2. Potential to support micro and small enterprises.

4.5.2 Factor Analysis: Identifying the most important factors of Business potential of IFB for Bank Officials.

Factor Analysis was conducted to identify the key factors influencing the **Business Potential of IFB for Bank Officials.**

Table 4.46- KMO and Bartlett's Test

KMO and Bartlett's Test		
Kaiser-Meyer-Olkin Measure of Sampling Adequacy.		**.750**
Bartlett's Test of Sphericity	Approx. Chi-Square	696.390
	df	45
	Sig.	.000

The KMO measure of sampling adequacy is **0.750** which indicates the present data is suitable for factor analysis. Similarly, Bartlett's test of sphericity is significant (p < 0.001); that explains existence of sufficient correlation between variables to proceed with the analysis.

Table 4.47- Total Variance Explained

Total Variance Explained									
Compo nent	Initial Eigenvalues			Extraction Sums of Squared Loadings			Rotation Sums of Squared Loadings		
	Total	% of Variance	Cumulat ive%	Total	% of Variance	Cumulat ive%	Total	% of Variance	Cumula tive%
1	2.848	**28.478**	28.478	2.848	28.478	28.478	2.333	23.330	23.330
2	1.214	**12.142**	40.620	1.214	12.142	40.620	1.645	16.449	39.779
3	1.156	**11.556**	52.177	1.156	11.556	52.177	1.240	12.398	52.177
4	.930	9.296	61.473						
5	.862	8.618	70.091						
6	.839	8.394	78.486						
7	.703	7.026	85.512						
8	.622	6.221	91.733						
9	.456	4.557	96.289						
10	.371	3.711	100.000						
Extraction Method: Principal Component Analysis.									

Findings and Interpretation: In the table provided, the output displays eight values associated with each linear component (factor) before extraction, after extraction, and after rotation. Prior to extraction, Output identified **3** linear components within the dataset. Following extraction and rotation, the primary factor **(Factor 1) explained 28.478% of the total variance, Factor 2 explained 12.142%, and Factor 3 explained 11.556%** of the total variance that could be extracted. The Total Variations Explained table indicates that among the 3 components, the first factor is the most significant and can be extracted.

Table 4.48- Rotated Component Matrix

Rotated Component Matrix[a]			
	Component		
	1	2	3
The customer base is large enough to start an alternative banking system.	.782	.204	.046
IFB System has the business potential in India.	.761	.040	.032
With time, customer base of IFB can be increased.	.645	.412	.056
IFB System can be developed in India for all.	.555	.158	-.167
IFBS needs to be governed by any specific regulatory body.	.464	.031	.315
IFSB should have transparency for business investments.	.169	.771	-.079
IFBS will be a good substitute for informal money lending institutions.	.172	.732	.054
IFSB will be able to get enough investment.	.210	-.247	.728
IFBS will be able to gain enough profit.	.294	-.181	-.611
IFBS will be able to fulfill needs of depositors, investors and borrowers.	.116	.428	.441
Extraction Method: Principal Component Analysis. Rotation Method: Varimax with Kaiser Normalization.			
a. Rotation converged in 3 iterations.			

Findings: Most Important factors of Business Potential of IFB for Bank Officials.

In the current study, Factor Analysis reveals the rotated factor loadings for the statements (variables) representing the most critical factors associated with the **Business Potential of IFB for Bank Officials.**

Factor- 1 (Potential Customer Base) includes following **5** variables

1. The customer base is large enough to start an alternative banking system.
2. **IFB** System has the business potential in India.
3. With time, customer base of **IFB** can be increased.
4. **IFB** System can be developed in India for all.
5. IFBS needs to be governed by any specific regulatory body.

Factor- 2 (Substitute for Informal Money Lending) includes following **2** variables

1. IFBS should have transparency for business investments.
2. IFBS will be a good substitute for informal money lending institutions.

Factor- 3 (Investment Potential for IFB) includes following **3** variables

1. IFBS will be able to get enough investment.
2. IFBS will be able to gain enough profit.
3. IFBS will be able to fulfill needs of depositors, investors and borrowers.

H₀₃.₁: There is no significant impact of Awareness Level on Business Potential of IFB from the perspective of General Public.

Table 4.49- ANOVA: Impact of Awareness Level on Business Potential (General Public)

ANOVAª						
Model		Sum of Squares	df	Mean Square	F	Sig.
1	Regression	56.671	1	56.671	39.187	.000ᵇ
	Residual	1784.588	1234	1.446		
	Total	1841.259	1235			
a. Dependent Variable: Business Potential						
b. Predictors: (Constant), Awareness Level						

The p-value (0.000) associated with F value came out be less than 0.05. It means there is significant impact of Awareness Level on the Business Potential and independent variables (IV) of our study **reliably predicts** the dependent variable (DV).

Table 4.50- Model Summary

Model Summary				
Model	R	R Square	Adjusted R Square	Std. Error of the Estimate
1	.175ª	.031	.030	1.203
a. Predictors: (Constant), Awareness Level				

The analysis explored the value of R square with the help of model summary table as given by the output. From the Model summary it was found that the proportion of explained variance as measured by R-Square was **(R2=0.031)** that signifies of about **03.1%** of the variance in **Business Potential** (dependent Variable) was explained by **Awareness Level** (independent variable).

Table 4.51- Coefficient

Model		Unstandardized Coefficients		Standardized Coefficients	t	Sig.
		B	Std. Error	Beta		
1	(Constant)	2.684	.126		21.270	.000
	Awareness Level	.242	.039	.175	6.260	.000
a. Dependent Variable: Business Potential						

Findings: Awareness Level: From the above table it was found the value of unstandardized-coefficients (Beta) is **0.242;** which is a positive value signifying that a 1-unit positive standard deviation change in it would bring **increase** in the standard deviation of dependent variable **Business Potential** by **0.242** unit.

Thus, on the ground that the value of coefficient is significant at .000 level, $H_{03.1}$ is rejected and concluded that **Awareness Level** have significant and positive impact on Business Potential in case of General Public's perspective.

$H_{03.2}$: *There is no significant impact of Awareness Level on Business Potential of IFB from the perspective of Bank Officials.*

Table 4.52- ANOVA: Impact of Awareness Level on Business Potential (Bank Officials)

Model		Sum of Squares	df	Mean Square	F	Sig.
1	Regression	.417	1	.417	.381	.537[b]
	Residual	474.269	434	1.093		
	Total	474.686	435			
a. Dependent Variable: Business Potential						
b. Predictors: (Constant), Awareness Level						

The p-value (0.537) associated with F value came out be more than 0.05. It means there is no significant impact of Awareness Level on Business Potential and independent variable (IV) of our study does not **reliably predict** the dependent variable (DV).

H_{03.3}: There is no significant impact of Acceptability Level on Business Potential of IFB from the perspective of General Public.

Table 4.53- ANOVA: Impact of Acceptability Level on Business Potential (General Public)

ANOVA[a]						
Model		Sum of Squares	df	Mean Square	F	Sig.
1	Regression	122.046	1	122.046	87.601	.000[b]
	Residual	1719.213	1234	1.393		
	Total	1841.259	1235			
a. Dependent Variable: Business Potential						
b. Predictors: (Constant), Acceptability Level						

The p-value (0.000) associated with F value came out be less than 0.05. It means there is significant impact of Acceptability Level on the Business Potential and independent variable (IV) of our study **reliably predicts** the dependent variable (DV).

Table 4.54- Model Summary

Model Summary				
Model	R	R Square	Adjusted R Square	Std. Error of the Estimate
1	.257[a]	.066	.066	1.180
a. Predictors: (Constant), Acceptability Level				

The analysis explored the value of R square with the help of model summary table as given by the output. From the Model summary it was found that the proportion of explained variance as measured by R-Square was **(R2=0.066)** that signifies of about **06.6%** of the variance in **Business Potential** (dependent Variable) was explained by **Acceptability Level** (independent variable).

Table 4.55- Coefficient

Coefficients[a]						
Model		Unstandardized Coefficients		Standardized Coefficients	t	Sig.
		B	Std. Error	Beta		
1	(Constant)	2.223	.135		16.485	.000
	Awareness Level	.371	.040	.257	9.360	.000
a. Dependent Variable: Business Potential						

Findings: Acceptability Level: From the above table it was found the value of unstandardized- coefficients (Beta) is **0.371;** which is a positive value signifying that a 1-unit positive standard deviation change in it would bring **increase** in the standard deviation of dependent variable **Business Potential** by 0.371 unit.

Thus, on the ground that the value of coefficient is significant at **.000** level, $H_{03.3}$ is rejected and concluded that **Acceptability Level** have significant and positive impact on **Business Potential** in case of General Public's perspective.

$H_{03.4}$: There is no significant impact of Acceptability Level on Business Potential of IFB from the perspective of Bank Officials.

Table 4.56- ANOVA: Impact of Acceptability Level on Business Potential (Bank Officials)

ANOVA[a]						
Model		Sum of Squares	df	Mean Square	F	Sig.
1	Regression	22.460	1	22.460	21.555	.000[b]
	Residual	452.225	434	1.042		
	Total	474.686	435			
a. Dependent Variable: Business Potential						
b. Predictors: (Constant), Acceptability Level						

The p-value (0.000) associated with F value came out be less than 0.05. It means there is significant impact of Acceptability Level on the Business Potential and independent variable (IV) of our study **reliably predicts** the dependent variable (DV).

Table 4.57- Model Summary

Model Summary				
Model	R	R Square	Adjusted R Square	Std. Error of the Estimate
1	.218[a]	.047	.045	1.021
a. Predictors: (Constant), Acceptability Level				

The analysis explored the value of R square with the help of model summary table as given by the output. From the Model summary it was found that the proportion of explained variance as measured by R-Square was **(R2=0.047)** that signifies of about **04.7%** of the variance in **Business Potential** (dependent variable) was explained by **Acceptability Level** (independent variable).

Table 4.58- Coefficient

Coefficients[a]						
Model		Unstandardized Coefficients		Standardized Coefficients	t	Sig.
		B	Std. Error	Beta		
1	(Constant)	2.663	.149		17.826	.000
	Awareness Level	.206	.044	.218	4.643	.000
a. Dependent Variable: Business Potential						

Findings: Acceptability Level: From the above table it was found the value of unstandardized- coefficients (Beta) is **0.206;** which is a positive value signifying that a 1-unit positive standard deviation change in it would bring **increase** in the standard deviation of dependent variable **Business Potential** by **0.206** unit.

Thus, on the ground that the value of coefficient is significant at **.000** level, $H_{03.4}$ is rejected and concluded that **Acceptability Level** have significant and positive impact on **Business Potential** in case of Bank Official's perspective.

$H_{03.5}$: *There is no significant difference between Male and Female Respondents among General Public regarding Business Potential of IFB.*

Table 4.59- Chi Square Tests: Gender wise Business Potential (General Public)

Chi-Square Tests			
	Value	df	Asymp. Sig. (2-sided)
Pearson Chi-Square	7.892[a]	4	.096

Findings and Interpretation: As per the Chi Square Tests, Pearson Chi-Square comes out to be insignificant (p value .096<.05). It means that there is no significant difference between Male and Female respondents among General Public regarding Business Potential of IFB. Therefore $H_{03.5}$ is accepted.

$H_{03.6}$: *There is no significant difference between Government Bank and Private Bank Respondents among Bank Officials regarding Business Potential of IFB.*

Table 4.60- Chi Square Tests: Gender wise Business Potential (Bank Officials)

Chi-Square Tests			
	Value	df	Asymptotic Significance (2-sided)
Pearson Chi-Square	1.012[a]	4	.908

Findings and Interpretation: As per the Chi Square Tests, Pearson Chi-Square comes out to be insignificant (p value .908<.05). It means that there is no significant difference between Government Bank and Private Bank respondents among Bank Officials regarding Business Potential of IFB. Therefore $H_{03.6}$ is accepted.

4.6 Research Objective 4: To identify the impact of Religion on Investing Behavior of Respondents.

$H_{04.1}$: There is no significant difference between Investing Behavior of Respondents and their Religions.

$H_{04.1.1}$: There is no significant difference between Respondents' Investing Behavior and their Religion regarding variable that emphasizes on social activities.

Table 4.61- Chi-Square Tests: Difference between Religion and Investing Behavior (Emphasizes on social activities)

Chi-Square Tests			
	Value	df	Asymptotic Significance (2-sided)
Pearson Chi-Square	103.033[a]	8	.000

Findings and Interpretation: As per the Chi Square Tests, Pearson Chi-Square comes out to be significant (p value .000<.05). It means that there is significant difference between consumers' Investing Behavior and their Religion regarding variable that emphasizes on social activities. Therefore $H_{04.1.1}$ is rejected.

Table 4.62- Crosstab: Emphasizes on social activities

Crosstab						
			Emphasizes on social activities			
			Neutral	Agree	Strongly Agree	Total
Religion	Hindu	Count	106	347	151	604
		% within	17.5%	57.5%	25.0%	100.0%
	Muslim	Count	92	190	229	511
		% within	18.0%	37.2%	44.8%	100.0%

	Christian	Count	2	35	5	42
		% within	4.8%	83.3%	11.9%	100.0%
	Sikh	Count	3	18	7	28
		% within	10.7%	64.3%	25.0%	100.0%
	Other	Count	5	43	3	51
		% within	9.8%	84.3%	5.9%	100.0%
	Total	Count	208	633	395	1236
		% within	16.8%	51.2%	32.0%	100.0%

Findings and Interpretation: It can be seen that majority of the respondents from all the religions (**Hindus, Muslims, Christians, Sikhs and Other**) agreed and strongly agreed that **banking system should** emphasize on social activities.

$H_{04.1.2}$: *There is no significant difference between Respondents' Investing Behavior and their Religion regarding variable that works on the principle of Prohibition of excessive risk/uncertainty.*

Table 4.63- Chi-Square Tests: Difference between Religion and Investing Behavior (Prohibition of excessive risk/uncertainty)

Chi-Square Tests			
	Value	df	Asymptotic Significance (2-sided)
Pearson Chi-Square	202.255[a]	8	.000

Findings and Interpretation: As per the Chi Square Tests, Pearson Chi-Square comes out to be significant (p value .000<.05). It means that there is significant difference between consumers' Investing Behavior and their Religion regarding variable that works on the principle of Prohibition of excessive risk/uncertainty. Therefore $H_{04.1.2}$ is rejected.

Table 4.64- Crosstab: That works on the principle of Prohibition of excessive risk/uncertainty

Crosstab						
			That works on the principle of Prohibition of excessive risk/ uncertainty.			
			Neutral	Agree	Strongly Agree	Total
Religion	Hindu	Count	20	452	132	604
		% within	3.3%	74.8%	21.9%	100.0%

			59	176	276	511
	Muslim	Count	59	176	276	511
		% within	11.5%	34.4%	54.0%	100.0%
	Christian	Count	0	31	11	42
		% within	0.0%	73.8%	26.2%	100.0%
	Sikh	Count	1	21	6	28
		% within	3.6%	75.0%	21.4%	100.0%
	Other	Count	0	35	16	51
		% within	0.0%	68.6%	31.4%	100.0%
Total		Count	80	715	441	1236
		% within	6.5%	57.8%	35.7%	100.0%

The above table shows that there are total 1236 respondents (General Public). The religion wise break-up of these respondents when asked about their readiness in investing a bank-That works on the principle of Prohibition of excessive risk/uncertainty-is as follows-

- **Hindu-** In this case, 21.9% respondents have strongly agreed, 74.8% have agreed and 3.3% were neutral.

- **Muslim-** In this case, 54% respondents have strongly agreed, 34.4% have agreed and 11.5% were neutral.

- **Christian-** In this case, 26.2% respondents have strongly agreed, 73.8% have agreed and 0.0% were neutral.

- **Sikh-** In this case, 21.4% respondents have strongly agreed, 75% have agreed and 3.6% were neutral.

- **Other-** In this case, 31.4% respondents have strongly agreed, 68.6% have agreed and 0.0% were neutral.

$H_{04.1.3}$: *There is no significant difference between Respondents' Investing Behavior and their Religion regarding variable that only allows the transactions that are backed by a tangible asset.*

Table 4.65- Chi-Square Tests: Difference between Religion and Investing Behavior (Transactions that are backed by a tangible asset)

Chi-Square Tests			
	Value	df	Asymptotic Significance (2-sided)
Pearson Chi-Square	158.408[a]	16	.000

Findings and Interpretation: As per the Chi Square Tests, Pearson Chi-Square comes out to be significant (p value .000<.05). It means that there is a significant difference between consumers' Investing Behavior and their Religion regarding variable that only allows the transactions that are backed by a tangible asset. Therefore $H_{04.1.3}$ is rejected.

Table 4.66- Crosstab: Only allows the transactions that are backed by a tangible asset

			\multicolumn{5}{	c	}{Only allows the transactions that are backed by a tangible asset.}	
			Strongly Disagree	Disagree	Neutral	Agree	Strongly Agree	Total
Religion	Hindu	Count	38	118	250	88	110	604
		% within	6.3%	19.5%	41.4%	14.6%	18.2%	100.0%
	Muslim	Count	76	50	94	147	144	511
		% within	14.9%	9.8%	18.4%	28.8%	28.2%	100.0%
	Christian	Count	1	6	15	18	2	42
		% within	2.4%	14.3%	35.7%	42.9%	4.8%	100.0%
	Sikh	Count	0	8	11	6	3	28
		% within	0.0%	28.6%	39.3%	21.4%	10.7%	100.0%
	Other	Count	3	9	17	18	4	51
		% within	5.9%	17.6%	33.3%	35.3%	7.8%	100.0%
	Total	Count	118	191	387	277	263	1236
		% within	9.5%	15.5%	31.3%	22.4%	21.3%	100.0%

The above table shows that there were total 1236 respondents (General Public). The religion wise break-up of these respondents when asked about their readiness in investing in a bank that only allows the transactions that are backed by a tangible asset- is as follows-

- **Hindu-** In this case, 18.2% respondents have strongly agreed, 14.6% respondents have agreed, 41.4% respondents were neutral, 19.5% respondents have disagreed and 6.3% respondents have strongly disagreed.

- **Muslim-** In this case, 28.2% respondents have strongly agreed, 28.8% respondents have agreed, 18.4% respondents were neutral, 9.8% respondents have disagreed and 14.9% respondents have strongly disagreed.

- **Christian-** In this case, 4.8% respondents have strongly agreed, 42.9% respondents have agreed and 35.7% respondents were neutral, 14.3% respondents have disagreed and 2.4% respondents have strongly disagreed.

- **Sikh-** In this case, 4.8% respondents have strongly agreed, 42.9% respondents have agreed, 35.7% respondents were neutral, 14.3% respondents have disagreed and 2.4% respondents have strongly disagreed.

- **Other-** In this case, 7.8% respondents have strongly agreed, 35.3% respondents have agreed, 33.3% respondents were neutral, 17.6% respondents have disagreed and 5.9% respondents have strongly disagreed.

$H_{04.1.4}$: There is no significant difference between Respondents' Investing Behavior and their Religion regarding variable that does not approve financing of alcohol.

Table 4.67- Chi-Square Tests: Difference between Religion and Investing Behavior (Does not approve financing of alcohol)

Chi-Square Tests			
	Value	df	Asymptotic Significance (2-sided)
Pearson Chi-Square	758.604[a]	16	.000

Findings and Interpretation: As per the Chi Square Tests, Pearson Chi-Square comes out to be significant (p value .000<.05). It means that there is significant difference between consumers' Investing Behavior and their Religion regarding variable that does not approve financing of alcohol. Therefore $H_{04.1.4}$ is rejected.

Table 4.68- Crosstab: Does not approve financing of alcohol

Crosstab								
			Does not approve financing of alcohol.					
			Strongly Disagree	Disagree	Neutral	Agree	Strongly Agree	Total
Religion	Hindu	Count	130	261	157	56	0	604
		% within	21.5%	43.2%	26.0%	9.3%	0.0%	100.0%
	Muslim	Count	0	0	98	246	167	511
		% within	0.0%	0.0%	19.2%	48.1%	32.7%	100.0%
	Christian	Count	2	7	9	24	0	42

			4.8%	16.7%	21.4%	57.1%	0.0%	100.0%
	Sikh	Count	3	18	5	2	0	28
		% within	10.7%	64.3%	17.9%	7.1%	0.0%	100.0%
	Other	Count	9	13	14	15	0	51
		% within	17.6%	25.5%	27.5%	29.4%	0.0%	100.0%
Total		Count	144	299	283	343	167	1236
		% within	11.7%	24.2%	22.9%	27.8%	13.5%	100.0%

The above table shows that there are total 1236 respondents (General Public). The religion wise break-up of these respondents when asked about their readiness in investing in a bank that does not approve financing of alcohol- is as follows-

- **Hindu-** In this case, 0.0% respondents have strongly agreed, 9.3% respondents have agreed, 26.0% respondents were neutral, 43.2% respondents have disagreed and 21.5% respondents have strongly disagreed.

- **Muslim-** In this case, 32.7% respondents have strongly agreed, 48.1% respondents have agreed, 19.2% respondents were neutral, 0% respondents have disagreed and 0% respondents have strongly disagreed.

- **Christian-** In this case, 0% respondents have strongly agreed, 57.1% respondents have agreed and 21.4% respondents were neutral, 16.7% respondents have disagreed and 4.8% respondents have strongly disagreed.

- **Sikh-** In this case, 0% respondents have strongly agreed, 7.1% respondents have agreed, 17.9% respondents were neutral, 64.3% respondents have disagreed and 10.7% respondents have strongly disagreed.

- **Other-** In this case, 0.0% respondents have strongly agreed, 29.4% respondents have agreed, 27.5% respondents were neutral, 25.5% respondents have disagreed and 17.6% respondents have strongly disagreed.

$H_{04.1.5}$: *There is no significant difference between Respondents' Investing Behavior and their Religion regarding variable that does not approve financing of pork.*

Table 4.69- Chi-Square Tests: Difference between Religion and Investing Behavior (Does not approve financing of pork)

Chi-Square Tests			
	Value	df	Asymptotic Significance (2-sided)
Pearson Chi-Square	1149.452[a]	16	.000

Findings and Interpretation: As per the Chi Square Tests, Pearson Chi-Square comes out to be significant (p value .000<.05). It means that there is significant difference between consumers' Investing Behavior and their Religion regarding variable that does not approve financing of pork. Therefore $H_{04.1.5}$ is rejected.

Table 4.70- Crosstab: Does not approve financing of pork

			\multicolumn{5}{c}{Does not approve financing of pork.}	
			Strongly Disagree	Disagree	Neutral	Agree	Strongly Agree	Total
Religion	Hindu	Count	473	69	6	56	0	604
		% within	78.3%	11.4%	1.0%	9.3%	0.0%	100.0%
	Muslim	Count	0	0	0	288	223	511
		% within	0.0%	0.0%	0.0%	56.4%	43.6%	100.0%
	Christian	Count	11	0	0	31	0	42
		% within	26.2%	0.0%	0.0%	73.8%	0.0%	100.0%
	Sikh	Count	22	2	2	2	0	28
		% within	78.6%	7.1%	7.1%	7.1%	0.0%	100.0%
	Other	Count	14	7	10	20	0	51
		% within	27.5%	13.7%	19.6%	39.2%	0.0%	100.0%
Total		Count	520	78	18	397	223	1236
		% within	42.1%	6.3%	1.5%	32.1%	18.0%	100.0%

Table header: **Crosstab**

The above table shows that there are total 1236 respondents (General Public). The religion wise break-up of these respondents when asked about their readiness in investing in a bank that does not approve financing of pork- is as follows-

- **Hindu-** In this case, 0.0% respondents have strongly agreed, 9.3% respondents have agreed, 1.0% respondents were neutral, 11.4% respondents have disagreed and 78.3% respondents have strongly disagreed.

- **Muslim-** In this case, 43.6% respondents have strongly agreed, 56.4% respondents have agreed, 0% respondents were neutral, 0% respondents have disagreed and 0% respondents have strongly disagreed.

- **Christian-** In this case, 0% respondents have strongly agreed, 73.8% respondents have agreed and 0% respondents were neutral, 0% respondents have disagreed and 26.2% respondents have strongly disagreed.

- **Sikh-** In this case, 0% respondents have strongly agreed, 7.1% respondents have agreed, 7.1% respondents were neutral, 7.1% respondents have disagreed and 78.6% respondents have strongly disagreed.

- **Other-** In this case, 0.0% respondents have strongly agreed, 39.2% respondents have agreed, 19.2% respondents were neutral, 13.7% respondents have disagreed and 27.5% respondents have strongly disagreed.

$H_{04.1.6}$: **There is no significant difference between Respondents' Investing Behavior and their Religion regarding variable that does not approve financing of ammunitions.**

Table 4.71- Chi-Square Tests: Difference between Religion and Investing Behavior

(Does not approve financing of ammunitions)

Chi-Square Tests			
	Value	df	Asymptotic Significance (2-sided)
Pearson Chi-Square	986.360[a]	16	.000

Findings and Interpretation: As per the Chi Square Tests, Pearson Chi-Square comes out to be significant (p value .000<.05). It means that there is significant difference between consumers' Investing Behavior and their Religion regarding variable that does not approve financing of ammunitions. Therefore $H_{04.1.6}$ is rejected.

Table 4.72- Crosstab: Does not approve financing of ammunitions

Crosstab								
			Does not approve financing of ammunitions					
			Strongly Disagree	Disagree	Neutral	Agree	Strongly Agree	Total
Religion	Hindu	Count	314	143	90	57	0	604
		% within	52.0%	23.7%	14.9%	9.4%	0.0%	100.0%
	Muslim	Count	0	0	82	404	25	511
		% within	0.0%	0.0%	16.0%	79.1%	4.9%	100.0%
	Christian	Count	1	11	30	0	0	42

		% within	2.4%	26.2%	71.4%	0.0%	0.0%	100.0%
	Sikh	Count	3	21	0	4	0	28
		% within	10.7%	75.0%	0.0%	14.3%	0.0%	100.0%
	Other	Count	1	20	14	16	0	51
		% within	2.0%	39.2%	27.5%	31.4%	0.0%	100.0%
Total		Count	319	195	216	481	25	1236
		% within	25.8%	15.8%	17.5%	38.9%	2.0%	100.0%

The above table shows that there are total 1236 respondents (General Public). The religion wise break-up of these respondents when asked about their readiness in investing in a bank that does not approve financing of ammunitions- is as follows-

- **Hindu-** In this case, 0.0% respondents have strongly agreed, 9.4% respondents have agreed, 14.9% respondents were neutral, 23.7% respondents have disagreed and 52.0% respondents have strongly disagreed.

- **Muslim-** In this case, 4.9% respondents have strongly agreed, 79.1% respondents have agreed, 16.0% respondents were neutral, 0.0% respondents have disagreed and 0.0% respondents have strongly disagreed.

- **Christian-** In this case, 0.0% respondents have strongly agreed, 0.0% respondents have agreed, 71.4% respondents were neutral, 26.2% respondents have disagreed and 2.4% respondents have strongly disagreed.

- **Sikh-** In this case, 0.0% respondents have strongly agreed, 14.3% respondents have agreed, 0.0% respondents were neutral, 75.0% respondents have disagreed and 10.7% respondents have strongly disagreed.

- **Other-** In this case, 0.0% respondents have strongly agreed, 31.4% respondents have agreed, 27.5% respondents were neutral, 39.2% respondents have disagreed and 2.0% respondents have strongly disagreed.

4.7 Research Objective 5: To identify the influence of demographic variables (Age, Gender, Educational Qualifications, Occupation and Monthly Income) on Investing Behavior of Respondents.

H$_{05}$: There is no significant difference between Respondents' Investing Behavior and their demographic variables (Age, Gender, Education, Occupation and Monthly Income).

4.7.1 Chi Square Analysis: Difference between Respondents' Investing Behavior and their Age.

$H_{05.1}$: *There is no significant difference between Respondents' Investing Behavior and their Age.*

$H_{05.1.1}$: *There is no significant difference between Respondents' Investing Behavior and their Age regarding variable- Tobacco/Alcohol products.*

Table 4.73- Chi Square Tests: Difference between Investing Behavior and Age (Tobacco/Alcohol Products)

Chi-Square Tests			
	Value	df	Asymptotic Significance (2-sided)
Pearson Chi-Square	21.592[a]	8	.006

Findings and Interpretation: As per the Chi Square Tests, Pearson Chi-Square comes out to be significant (p value .006<.05). It means that there is significant difference between consumers' Investing Behavior and their Age regarding variable- Tobacco/Alcohol products. Therefore $H_{05.1.1}$ is rejected.

Table 4.74- Crosstab: Tobacco/Alcohol Products

Crosstab							
			Tobacco/Alcohol products					Total
			Strongly Disagree	Disagree	Neutral	Agree	Strongly Agree	Total
Age	21 years to 30	Count	9	21	9	86	29	154
		% within	5.8%	13.6%	5.8%	55.8%	18.8%	100.0%
	31 years to 40	Count	34	114	40	315	115	618
		% within	5.5%	18.4%	6.5%	51.0%	18.6%	100.0%
	41 years to 50	Count	25	83	29	282	45	464
		% within	5.4%	17.9%	6.3%	60.8%	9.7%	100.0%
Total		Count	68	218	78	683	189	1236
		% within	5.5%	17.6%	6.3%	55.3%	15.3%	100.0%

The above table shows that there are total 1236 respondents (General Public). The age wise break-up of these respondents when asked about their unwillingness for investing in Tobacco/Alcohol products- is as follows-

- **21 to 30 years-** In this case, 18.8% respondents have strongly agreed, 55.8% respondents have agreed, 5.8% respondents were neutral, 13.6% respondents have disagreed and 5.8% respondents have strongly disagreed.

- **31 to 40 years-** In this case, 18.6% respondents have strongly agreed, 51.0% respondents have agreed, 6.5% respondents were neutral, 18.4% respondents have disagreed and 5.5% respondents have strongly disagreed.

- **41 to 50 years-** In this case, 9.7% respondents have strongly agreed, 60.8% respondents have agreed, 6.3% respondents were neutral, 17.9% respondents have disagreed and 5.4% respondents have strongly disagreed.

$H_{05.1.2}$: There is no significant difference between Respondents' Investing Behavior and their Age regarding variable- All Non-Vegetarian Products.

Table 4.75- Chi Square Tests: Difference between Investing Behavior and Age (All Non-Vegetarian Products)

Chi-Square Tests			
	Value	df	Asymptotic Significance (2-sided)
Pearson Chi-Square	15.799[a]	8	.045

Findings and Interpretation: As per the Chi Square Tests, Pearson Chi-Square comes out to be significant (p value .045<.05). It means that there is significant difference between consumers' Investing Behavior and their Age regarding variable- All Non-Vegetarian Products. Therefore $H_{05.1.2}$ is rejected.

Table 4.76- Crosstab: All Non-Vegetarian Products

Crosstab							
			All Non-Vegetarian Products				
			Strongly Disagree	Disagree	Neutral	Agree	Strongly Agree	Total
Age	21 years to 30	Count	19	73	13	42	7	154
		% within	12.3%	47.4%	8.4%	27.3%	4.5%	100.0%
	31 years to 40	Count	91	285	71	145	26	618
		% within	14.7%	46.1%	11.5%	23.5%	4.2%	100.0%

41 years to 50	Count	35	221	55	129	24	464
	% within	7.5%	47.6%	11.9%	27.8%	5.2%	100.0%
Total	Count	145	579	139	316	57	1236
	% within	11.7%	46.8%	11.2%	25.6%	4.6%	100.0%

The above table shows that there are total 1236 respondents (General Public). The age wise break-up of these respondents when asked about their unwillingness for investing in All Non-Vegetarian Products- is as follows-

- **21 to 30 years-** In this case, 4.5% respondents have strongly agreed, 27.3% respondents have agreed, 8.4% respondents were neutral, 47.4% respondents have disagreed and 12.3% respondents have strongly disagreed.

- **31 to 40 years-** In this case, 4.2% respondents have strongly agreed, 23.5% respondents have agreed, 11.5% respondents were neutral, 46.1% respondents have disagreed and 14.7% respondents have strongly disagreed.

- **41 to 50 years-** In this case, 5.2% respondents have strongly agreed, 27.8% respondents have agreed, 11.9% respondents were neutral, 47.6% respondents have disagreed and 7.5% respondents have strongly disagreed.

$H_{05.1.3}$: There is no significant difference between Respondents' Investing Behavior and their Age regarding variable- Arms and Ammunition.

Table 4.77- Chi Square Tests: Difference between Investing Behavior and Age (Arms and Ammunition)

Chi-Square Tests			
	Value	df	Asymptotic Significance (2-sided)
Pearson Chi-Square	10.304[a]	8	.244

Findings and Interpretation: As per the Chi Square Tests, Pearson Chi-Square comes out to be insignificant (p value .244<.05). It means that there is no significant difference between consumers' Investing Behavior and their Age regarding variable- Arms and Ammunition. Therefore $H_{05.1.3}$ is accepted.

$H_{05.1.4}$: There is no significant difference between Respondents' Investing Behavior and their Age regarding variable- Non-Environment Friendly Products.

Table 4.78- Chi Square Tests: Difference between Investing Behavior and Age (Non-Environment Friendly Products)

Chi-Square Tests			
	Value	df	Asymptotic Significance (2-sided)
Pearson Chi-Square	37.684[a]	8	.000

Findings and Interpretation: As per the Chi Square Tests, Pearson Chi-Square comes out to be significant (p value .000<.05). It means that there is significant difference between consumers' Investing Behavior and their Age regarding variable- Non-Environment Friendly Products. Therefore $H_{05.1.3}$ is rejected.

Table 4.79- Crosstab: Non-Environment Friendly Products

Crosstab								
			Non-Environment Friendly Products					
			Strongly Disagree	Disagree	Neutral	Agree	Strongly Agree	Total
Age	21 years to 30	Count	7	35	26	43	43	154
		% within	4.5%	22.7%	16.9%	27.9%	27.9%	100.0%
	31 years to 40	Count	33	145	121	149	170	618
		% within	5.3%	23.5%	19.6%	24.1%	27.5%	100.0%
	41 years to 50	Count	30	118	93	160	63	464
		% within	6.5%	25.4%	20.0%	34.5%	13.6%	100.0%
Total		Count	70	298	240	352	276	1236
		% within	5.7%	24.1%	19.4%	28.5%	22.3%	100.0%

The above table shows that there are total 1236 respondents (General Public). The age wise break-up of these respondents when asked about their unwillingness for investing in Non-Environment Friendly Products- is as follows-

- **21 to 30 years-** In this case, 27.9% respondents have strongly agreed, 27.9% respondents have agreed, 16.9% respondents were neutral, 22.7% respondents have disagreed and 4.5% respondents have strongly disagreed.

- **31 to 40 years-** In this case, 27.5% respondents have strongly agreed, 24.1% respondents have agreed, 19.6% respondents were neutral, 23.5% respondents have disagreed and 5.3% respondents have strongly disagreed.

- **41 to 50 years-** In this case, 13.6% respondents have strongly agreed, 34.5% respondents have agreed, 20.0% respondents were neutral, 25.4% respondents have disagreed and 6.5% respondents have strongly disagreed.

$H_{05.1.5}$: There is no significant difference between Respondents' Investing Behavior and their Age regarding variable- Products that involves animal cruelty.

Table 4.80- Chi Square Tests: Difference between Investing Behavior and Age (Products that involves animal cruelty)

Chi-Square Tests			
	Value	df	Asymptotic Significance (2-sided)
Pearson Chi-Square	14.778[a]	4	.005

Findings and Interpretation: As per the Chi Square Tests, Pearson Chi-Square comes out to be significant (p value .005<.05). It means that there is significant difference between consumers' Investing Behavior and their Age regarding variable- Products that involves Animal Cruelty. Therefore $H_{05.1.5:}$ is rejected.

Table 4.81- Crosstab: Products that involves animal cruelty

Crosstab						
			Products that involves animal cruelty			
			Neutral	Agree	Strongly Agree	Total
Age	21 years to 30	Count	15	80	59	154
		% within	9.7%	51.9%	38.3%	100.0%
	31 years to 40	Count	68	319	231	618
		% within	11.0%	51.6%	37.4%	100.0%
	41 years to 50	Count	49	288	127	464
		% within	10.6%	62.1%	27.4%	100.0%
Total		Count	132	687	417	1236
		% within	10.7%	55.6%	33.7%	100.0%

The above table shows that there are total 1236 respondents (General Public). The age wise break-up of these respondents when asked about their unwillingness for investing in products that involves Animal Cruelty- is as follows-

- **21 to 30 years-** In this case, 38.3% respondents have strongly agreed, 51.9% respondents have agreed, 9.7% respondents were neutral.
- **31 to 40 years-** In this case, 37.4% respondents have strongly agreed, 51.6% respondents have agreed, 11.0% respondents were neutral.
- **41 to 50 years-** In this case, 27.4% respondents have strongly agreed, 62.1% respondents have agreed, 10.6% respondents were neutral.

4.7.2 Chi Square Analysis: Difference between Respondents' Investing Behavior and their Genders.

H$_{05.2}$: There is no significant difference between Respondents' Investing Behavior and their Gender.

H$_{05.2.1}$: There is no significant difference between Respondents' Investing Behavior and their Gender regarding variable- Tobacco/Alcohol products.

Table 4.82- Chi Square Tests: Difference between Investing Behavior and Gender (Tobacco/Alcohol products)

Chi-Square Tests			
	Value	df	Asymptotic Significance (2-sided)
Pearson Chi-Square	5.729[a]	4	.220

Findings and Interpretation: As per the Chi Square Tests, Pearson Chi-Square comes out to be insignificant (p value .220<.05). It means that there is no significant difference between respondents' Investing Behavior and their Gender regarding variable- Tobacco/Alcohol products. Therefore H$_{05.2.1}$ is accepted.

H$_{05.2.2}$: There is no significant difference between Respondents' Investing Behavior and their Gender regarding variable- All non-vegetarian Products.

Table 4.83- Chi Square Tests: Difference between Investing Behavior and Gender (All non-vegetarian Products)

Chi-Square Tests			
	Value	df	Asymptotic Significance (2-sided)
Pearson Chi-Square	3.126[a]	4	.537

Findings and Interpretation: As per the Chi Square Tests, Pearson Chi-Square comes out to be insignificant (p value .537<.05). It means that there is no significant difference between respondents' Investing Behavior and their Gender regarding variable- All Non-Vegetarian Products. Therefore $H_{05.2.2}$ is accepted.

$H_{05.2.3}$: There is no significant difference between Respondents' Investing Behavior and their Gender regarding variable- Arms and Ammunition.

Table 4.84- Chi Square Tests: Difference between Investing Behavior and Gender (Arms and Ammunition)

Chi-Square Tests			
	Value	df	Asymptotic Significance (2-sided)
Pearson Chi-Square	6.571[a]	4	.160

Findings and Interpretation: As per the Chi Square Tests, Pearson Chi-Square comes out to be insignificant (p value .160<.05). It means that there is no significant difference between respondents' Investing Behavior and their Gender regarding variable- Arms and Ammunition. Therefore $H_{05.2.3}$ is accepted.

$H_{05.2.4}$: There is no significant difference between Respondents' Investing Behavior and their Gender regarding variable- Non-Environment Friendly Products.

Table 4.85- Chi Square Tests: Difference between Investing Behavior and Gender (Non-Environment Friendly Products)

Chi-Square Tests			
	Value	df	Asymptotic Significance (2-sided)
Pearson Chi-Square	.638[a]	4	.959

Findings and Interpretation: As per the Chi Square Tests, Pearson Chi-Square comes out to be insignificant (p value .959<.05). It means that there is no significant difference between respondents' Investing Behavior and their Gender regarding variable- Non-Environment Friendly Products. Therefore $H_{05.2.4}$ is accepted.

$H_{05.2.5}$: There is no significant difference between Respondents' Investing Behavior and their Gender regarding variable- Products that involves Animal Cruelty.

123

Table 4.86- Chi Square Tests: Difference between Investing Behavior and Gender (Products that involves Animal Cruelty)

Chi-Square Tests			
	Value	df	Asymptotic Significance (2-sided)
Pearson Chi-Square	.194[a]	2	.907

Findings and Interpretation: As per the Chi Square Tests, Pearson Chi-Square comes out to be insignificant (p value .907<.05). It means that there is no significant difference between respondents' Investing Behavior and their Gender regarding variable- Products that involves Animal Cruelty. Therefore $H_{05.2.5}$ is accepted.

4.7.3 Chi Square Analysis: Difference between Respondents' Investing Behavior and their Educational Qualifications.

$H_{05.3}$: There is no significant difference between Respondents' Investing Behavior and their Educational Qualifications.

$H_{05.3.1}$: There is no significant difference between Respondents' Investing Behavior and their Educational Qualifications regarding variable- Tobacco/Alcohol products.

Table 4.87- Chi Square Tests: Difference between Investing Behavior and Educational Qualifications (Tobacco/Alcohol products)

Chi-Square Tests			
	Value	Df	Asymptotic Significance (2-sided)
Pearson Chi-Square	33.314[a]	16	.007

Findings and Interpretation: As per the Chi Square Tests, Pearson Chi-Square comes out to be significant (p value .007<.05). It means that there is significant difference between respondents' Investing Behavior and their Educational Qualifications regarding variable- Tobacco/Alcohol products. Therefore $H_{05.3.1}$ is rejected.

Table 4.88- Crosstab: Tobacco/Alcohol products

Crosstab								
			Tobacco/Alcohol products					
			Strongly Disagree	Disagree	Neutral	Agree	Strongly Agree	Total
Educational	Graduation	Count	14	60	17	207	48	346

Qualifications		% within	4.0%	17.3%	4.9%	59.8%	13.9%	100.0%
	Post-Graduation	Count	34	88	29	251	71	473
		% within	7.2%	18.6%	6.1%	53.1%	15.0%	100.0%
	Professionally Qualified	Count	4	25	8	61	22	120
		% within	3.3%	20.8%	6.7%	50.8%	18.3%	100.0%
	Others	Count	16	45	20	158	48	287
		% within	5.6%	15.7%	7.0%	55.1%	16.7%	100.0%
	PhD	Count	0	0	4	6	0	10
		% within	0.0%	0.0%	40.0%	60.0%	0.0%	100.0%
Total		Count	68	218	78	683	189	1236
		% within	5.5%	17.6%	6.3%	55.3%	15.3%	100.0%

The above table shows that there are total 1236 respondents (General Public). The Educational Qualifications wise break-up of these respondents when asked about their unwillingness for investing in Tobacco/Alcohol products- is as follows-

- **Graduation-** In this case, 13.9% respondents have strongly agreed, 59.8% respondents have agreed, 4.9% respondents were neutral, 17.3% respondents have disagreed and 4.0% respondents have strongly disagreed.

- **Post-Graduation -** In this case, 15.0% respondents have strongly agreed, 53.1% respondents have agreed, 6.1% respondents were neutral, 18.6% respondents have disagreed and 7.2% respondents have strongly disagreed.

- **Professionally Qualified-** In this case, 18.3% respondents have strongly agreed, 50.8% respondents have agreed, 6.7% respondents were neutral, 20.8% respondents have disagreed and 3.3% respondents have strongly disagreed.

- **Others-** In this case, 16.7% respondents have strongly agreed, 55.1% respondents have agreed, 7.0% respondents were neutral, 15.7% respondents have disagreed and 5.6% respondents have strongly disagreed.

- **PhD-** In this case, 0.0% respondents have strongly agreed, 60.0% respondents have agreed, 40.0% respondents were neutral, 0.0% respondents have disagreed and0.0% respondents have strongly disagreed.

$H_{05.3.2}$: There is no significant difference between Respondents' Investing Behavior and their Educational Qualifications regarding variable- All non-vegetarian Products.

Table 4.89- Chi Square Test: Difference between Investing Behavior and Educational Qualifications (All non-vegetarian Products)

Chi-Square Tests			
	Value	df	Asymptotic Significance (2-sided)
Pearson Chi-Square	18.684[a]	16	.285

Findings and Interpretation: As per the Chi Square Tests, Pearson Chi-Square comes out to be insignificant (p value .285<.05). It means that there is no significant difference between respondents' Investing Behavior and their Educational Qualifications regarding variable- All Non-Vegetarian Products. Therefore $H_{05.3.2}$ is accepted.

$H_{05.3.3}$: *There is no significant difference between Respondents' Investing Behavior and their Educational Qualifications regarding variable- Arms and Ammunition.*

Table 4.90- Chi Square Tests: Difference between Investing Behavior and Educational Qualifications (Arms and Ammunition)

Chi-Square Tests			
	Value	df	Asymptotic Significance (2-sided)
Pearson Chi-Square	22.768[a]	16	.120

Findings and Interpretation: As per the Chi Square Tests, Pearson Chi-Square comes out to be insignificant (p value .120<.05). It means that there is no significant difference in respondents' Investing Behavior and their Educational Qualifications regarding variable- Arms and Ammunition. Therefore $H_{05.3.3}$ is accepted.

$H_{05.3.4}$: *There is no significant difference between Respondents' Investing Behavior and their Educational Qualifications regarding variable- Non-Environment Friendly Products.*

Table 4.91- Chi Square Tests: Difference between Investing Behavior and Educational Qualifications (Non-Environment Friendly Products)

Chi-Square Tests			
	Value	df	Asymptotic Significance (2-sided)
Pearson Chi-Square	22.278[a]	16	.134

Findings and Interpretation: As per the Chi Square Tests, Pearson Chi-Square comes out to be insignificant (p value .134<.05). It means there is no significant difference between respondents' Investing Behavior and their Educational Qualifications regarding variable-Non-Environment Friendly Products. Therefore $H_{05.3.4}$ is accepted.

$H_{05.3.5}$: *There is no significant difference between Respondents' Investing Behavior and their Educational Qualifications regarding variable- Products that involves animal cruelty.*

Table 4.92- Chi Square Tests: Difference between Investing Behavior and Educational Qualifications (Products that involves animal cruelty)

Chi-Square Tests			
	Value	df	Asymptotic Significance (2-sided)
Pearson Chi-Square	10.221[a]	8	.250

Findings and Interpretation: As per the Chi Square Tests, Pearson Chi-Square comes out to be insignificant (p value .250<.05). It means that there is no significant difference between respondents' Investing Behavior and their Educational Qualifications regarding variable-Products that involves animal cruelty. Therefore $H_{05.3.5}$ is accepted.

4.7.4 Chi Square Analysis: Difference between Respondents' Investing Behavior and their Occupation.

$H_{05.4}$: *There is no significant difference between Respondents' Investing Behavior and their Occupation.*

$H_{05.4.1}$: *There is no significant difference between Respondents' Investing Behavior and their Occupation regarding variable- Tobacco/Alcohol products.*

Table 4.93- Chi Square Tests: Difference between Investing Behavior and Occupation (Tobacco/Alcohol Products)

Chi-Square Tests			
	Value	df	Asymptotic Significance (2-sided)
Pearson Chi-Square	57.701[a]	12	.000

Findings and Interpretation: As per the Chi Square Tests, Pearson Chi-Square comes out to be significant (p value .000<.05). It means that there is significant difference between respondents' Investing Behavior and their Occupation regarding variable- Tobacco/Alcohol products. Therefore $H_{05.4.1}$ is rejected.

Table 4.94- Crosstab: Tobacco/Alcohol Products

			Tobacco/Alcohol products					
			Strongly Disagree	Disagree	Neutral	Agree	Strongly Agree	Total
Occupation	Private Job	Count	22	71	23	220	46	382
		% within	5.8%	18.6%	6.0%	57.6%	12.0%	100.0%
	Govern ment Job	Count	20	66	14	114	30	244
		% within	8.2%	27.0%	5.7%	46.7%	12.3%	100.0%
	Business	Count	19	65	36	327	106	553
		% within	3.4%	11.8%	6.5%	59.1%	19.2%	100.0%
	Others	Count	7	16	5	22	7	57
		% within	12.3%	28.1%	8.8%	38.6%	12.3%	100.0%
Total		Count	68	218	78	683	189	1236
		% within	5.5%	17.6%	6.3%	55.3%	15.3%	100.0%

The above table shows that there are total 1236 respondents (General Public). The Occupation wise break-up of these respondents when asked about their unwillingness for investing in Tobacco/Alcohol products- is as follows-

- **Private Job-** In this case, 12.0% respondents have strongly agreed, 57.6% respondents have agreed, 6.0% respondents were neutral, 18.6% respondents have disagreed and 5.8% respondents have strongly disagreed.

- **Government Job-** In this case, 12.3% respondents have strongly agreed, 46.7% respondents have agreed, 5.7% respondents were neutral, 27.0% respondents have disagreed and 8.2% respondents have strongly disagreed.

- **Business-** In this case, 19.2% respondents have strongly agreed, 59.1% respondents have agreed, 6.5% respondents were neutral, 11.8% respondents have disagreed and 3.4% respondents have strongly disagreed.

- **Others-** In this case, 12.3% respondents have strongly agreed, 38.6% respondents have agreed, 8.8% respondents were neutral, 28.1% respondents have disagreed and 12.3% respondents have strongly disagreed.

$H_{05.4.2}$**: There is no significant difference between Respondents' Investing Behavior and their Occupation regarding variable- All non-vegetarian Products.**

Table 4.95- Chi Square Tests: Difference between Investing Behavior and Occupation (All non-vegetarian Products)

Chi-Square Tests			
	Value	df	Asymptotic Significance (2-sided)
Pearson Chi-Square	129.275[a]	12	.000

Findings and Interpretation: As per the Chi Square Tests, Pearson Chi-Square comes out to be significant (p value .000<.05). It means that there is significant difference between respondents' Investing Behavior and their Occupation regarding variable- All Non-Vegetarian Products. Therefore $H_{05.4.2}$ is rejected.

Table 4.96- Crosstab: All non-vegetarian Products

Crosstab								
			All Non-Vegetarian Products					
			Strongly Disagree	Disagree	Neutral	Agree	Strongly Agree	Total
Occupation	Private Job	Count	32	184	41	110	15	382
		% within	8.4%	48.2%	10.7%	28.8%	3.9%	100.0%
	Govern ment Job	Count	13	80	43	82	26	244
		% within	5.3%	32.8%	17.6%	33.6%	10.7%	100.0%
	Business	Count	96	302	47	98	10	553
		% within	17.4%	54.6%	8.5%	17.7%	1.8%	100.0%
	Others	Count	4	13	8	26	6	57
		% within	7.0%	22.8%	14.0%	45.6%	10.5%	100.0%
Total		Count	145	579	139	316	57	1236
		% within	11.7%	46.8%	11.2%	25.6%	4.6%	100.0%

The above table shows that there are total 1236 respondents (General Public). The Occupation wise break-up of these respondents when asked about their unwillingness for investing in All Non-Vegetarian Products- is as follows-

- **Private Job-** In this case, 3.9% respondents have strongly agreed, 28.8% respondents have agreed, 10.7% respondents were neutral, 48.2% respondents have disagreed and 8.4% respondents have strongly disagreed.

- **Government Job-** In this case, 10.7% respondents have strongly agreed, 33.6% respondents have agreed, 17.6% respondents were neutral, 32.8% respondents have disagreed and 5.3% respondents have strongly disagreed.

- **Business-** In this case, 1.8% respondents have strongly agreed, 17.7% respondents have agreed, 8.5% respondents were neutral, 54.6% respondents have disagreed and 17.4% respondents have strongly disagreed.

- **Others-** In this case, 10.5% respondents have strongly agreed, 45.6% respondents have agreed, 14.0% respondents were neutral, 22.8% respondents have disagreed and 7.0% respondents have strongly disagreed.

$H_{05.4.3}$: *There is no significant difference between Respondents' Investing Behavior and their Occupation regarding variable- Arms and Ammunition.*

Table 4.97- Chi Square Tests: Difference between Investing Behavior and Occupation (Arms and Ammunition)

Chi-Square Tests			
	Value	df	Asymptotic Significance (2-sided)
Pearson Chi-Square	26.933[a]	12	.008

Findings and Interpretation: As per the Chi Square Tests, Pearson Chi-Square comes out to be significant (p value .008<.05). It means that there is significant difference between respondents' Investing Behavior and their Occupation regarding variable- Arms and Ammunition. Therefore $H_{05.4.3}$ is rejected.

Table 4.98- Crosstab: Arms and Ammunition

Crosstab			Arms and Ammunition					
			Strongly Disagree	Disagree	Neutral	Agree	Strongly Agree	Total
Occupation	Private Job	Count	66	238	67	7	4	382
		% within	17.3%	62.3%	17.5%	1.8%	1.0%	100.0%
	Government Job	Count	45	154	25	16	4	244
		% within	18.4%	63.1%	10.2%	6.6%	1.6%	100.0%
	Business	Count	76	358	96	18	5	553
		% within	13.7%	64.7%	17.4%	3.3%	0.9%	100.0%
	Others	Count	15	28	12	2	0	57

		% within	26.3%	49.1%	21.1%	3.5%	0.0%	100.0%
	Total	Count	202	778	200	43	13	1236
		% within	16.3%	62.9%	16.2%	3.5%	1.1%	100.0%

The above table shows that there are total 1236 respondents (General Public). The Occupation wise break-up of these respondents when asked about their unwillingness for investing in Arms and Ammunition- is as follows-

- **Private Job-** In this case, 1.0% respondents have strongly agreed, 1.8% respondents have agreed, 17.5% respondents were neutral, 62.3% respondents have disagreed and 17.3% respondents have strongly disagreed.

- **Government Job-** In this case, 1.6% respondents have strongly agreed, 6.6% respondents have agreed, 10.2% respondents were neutral, 63.1% respondents have disagreed and 18.4% respondents have strongly disagreed.

- **Business-** In this case, 0.9% respondents have strongly agreed, 3.3% respondents have agreed, 17.4% respondents were neutral, 64.7% respondents have disagreed and 13.7% respondents have strongly disagreed.

- **Others-** In this case, 0.0% respondents have strongly agreed, 3.5% respondents have agreed, 21.1% respondents were neutral, 49.1% respondents have disagreed and 26.3% respondents have strongly disagreed.

$H_{05.4.4}$: *There is no significant difference between Respondents' Investing Behavior and their Occupation regarding variable- Non-Environment Friendly Products.*

Table 4.99- Chi Square Tests: Difference between Investing Behavior and Occupation (Non-Environment Friendly Products)

Chi-Square Tests			
	Value	df	Asymptotic Significance (2-sided)
Pearson Chi-Square	37.303[a]	12	.000

Findings and Interpretation: As per the Chi Square Tests, Pearson Chi-Square comes out to be significant (p value .000<.05). It means that there is significant difference between respondents' Investing Behavior and their Occupation regarding variable- Non-Environment Friendly Products. Therefore $H_{05.4.4}$ is rejected.

Table 4.100- Crosstab: Non-Environment Friendly Products

			Non-Environment Friendly Products					
			Strongly Disagree	Disagree	Neutral	Agree	Strongly Agree	Total
Occupation	Private Job	Count	26	109	73	105	69	382
		% within	6.8%	28.5%	19.1%	27.5%	18.1%	100.0%
	Govern ment Job	Count	18	48	58	74	46	244
		% within	7.4%	19.7%	23.8%	30.3%	18.9%	100.0%
	Business	Count	19	129	94	157	154	553
		% within	3.4%	23.3%	17.0%	28.4%	27.8%	100.0%
	Others	Count	7	12	15	16	7	57
		% within	12.3%	21.1%	26.3%	28.1%	12.3%	100.0%
Total		Count	70	298	240	352	276	1236
		% within	5.7%	24.1%	19.4%	28.5%	22.3%	100.0%

The above table shows that there are total 1236 respondents (General Public). The Occupation wise break-up of these respondents when asked about their unwillingness for investing in Non-Environment Friendly Products- is as follows-

- **Private Job-** In this case, 18.1% respondents have strongly agreed, 27.5% respondents have agreed, 19.1% respondents were neutral, 28.5% respondents have disagreed and 6.8% respondents have strongly disagreed.

- **Government Job-** In this case, 18.9% respondents have strongly agreed, 30.3% respondents have agreed, 23.8% respondents were neutral, 19.7% respondents have disagreed and 7.4% respondents have strongly disagreed.

- **Business-** In this case, 27.8% respondents have strongly agreed, 28.4% respondents have agreed, 17.0% respondents were neutral, 23.3% respondents have disagreed and 3.4% respondents have strongly disagreed.

- **Others-** In this case, 12.3% respondents have strongly agreed, 28.1% respondents have agreed, 26.3% respondents were neutral, 21.1% respondents have disagreed and 12.3% respondents have strongly disagreed.

$H_{05.4.5}$: *There is no significant difference between Respondents' Investing Behavior and their Occupation regarding variable- Products that involves animal cruelty.*

Table 4.101- Chi Square Tests: Difference between Investing Behavior and Occupation (Products that involves animal cruelty)

Chi-Square Tests			
	Value	df	Asymptotic Significance (2-sided)
Pearson Chi-Square	37.094[a]	6	.000

Findings and Interpretation: As per the Chi Square Tests, Pearson Chi-Square comes out to be significant (p value .000<.05). It means that there is significant difference between respondents' Investing Behavior and their Occupation regarding variable- Products that involves Animal Cruelty. Therefore $H_{05.4.5}$ is rejected.

Table 4.102- Crosstab: Products that involves Animal Cruelty

Crosstab						
			Products that involves Animal Cruelty			
			Neutral	Agree	Strongly Agree	Total
Occupation	Private Job	Count	48	219	115	382
		% within	12.6%	57.3%	30.1%	100.0%
	Government Job	Count	43	125	76	244
		% within	17.6%	51.2%	31.1%	100.0%
	Business	Count	31	309	213	553
		% within	5.6%	55.9%	38.5%	100.0%
	Others	Count	10	34	13	57
		% within	17.5%	59.6%	22.8%	100.0%
Total		Count	132	687	417	1236
		% within	10.7%	55.6%	33.7%	100.0%

The above table shows that there are total 1236 respondents (General Public). The Occupation wise break-up of these respondents when asked about their unwillingness for investing in Products that involves Animal Cruelty- is as follows-

- **Private Job-** In this case, 30.1% respondents have strongly agreed, 57.3%

133

respondents have agreed, 12.6% respondents were neutral.

- **Government Job-** In this case, 31.1% respondents have strongly agreed, 51.2% respondents have agreed, 17.6% respondents were neutral.
- **Business-** In this case, 38.5% respondents have strongly agreed, 55.9% respondents have agreed, 5.6% respondents were neutral.
- **Others-** In this case, 22.8% respondents have strongly agreed, 59.6% respondents have agreed, 17.5% respondents were neutral.

4.7.5 Chi Square Analysis: Difference between Respondents' Investing Behavior and their Monthly Income.

$H_{05.5}$: *There is no significant difference between Respondents' Investing Behavior and their Monthly Income.*

$H_{05.5.1}$: *There is no significant difference between Respondents' Investing Behavior and their Monthly Income regarding variable- Tobacco/Alcohol products.*

Table 4.103- Chi Square Tests: Difference between Investing Behavior and Monthly Income (Tobacco/Alcohol Products)

Chi-Square Tests			
	Value	df	Asymptotic Significance (2-sided)
Pearson Chi-Square	31.771[a]	16	.011

Findings and Interpretation: As per the Chi Square Tests, Pearson Chi-Square comes out to be significant (p value .011<.05). It means that there is significant difference between respondents' Investing Behavior and their Monthly Income regarding variable-Tobacco/Alcohol products. Therefore $H_{05.5.1}$ is rejected.

Table 4.104- Crosstab: Tobacco/Alcohol Products

Crosstab								
			Tobacco/Alcohol products					
			Strongly Disagree	Disagree	Neutral	Agree	Strongly Agree	Total
Monthly Income	Below Rs. 25,000	Count	17	33	7	81	12	150
		% within	11.3%	22.0%	4.7%	54.0%	8.0%	100.0%
	Between Rs 25,001 to Rs. 50,000	Count	13	43	21	196	50	323
		% within	4.0%	13.3%	6.5%	60.7%	15.5%	100.0%

Between Rs 50,001 to Rs. 75,000	Count	12	39	12	111	38	212
	% within	5.7%	18.4%	5.7%	52.4%	17.9%	100.0%
Between Rs 75,001 to Rs. 1,00,000	Count	23	84	33	234	65	439
	% within	5.2%	19.1%	7.5%	53.3%	14.8%	100.0%
Above Rs. 1,00,000.	Count	3	19	5	61	24	112
	% within	2.7%	17.0%	4.5%	54.5%	21.4%	100.0%
Total	Count	68	218	78	683	189	1236
	% within	5.5%	17.6%	6.3%	55.3%	15.3%	100.0%

The above table shows that there are total 1236 respondents (General Public). The monthly incomewise break-up of these respondents when asked about their unwillingness for investing in Tobacco/Alcohol products- is as follows-

- **Below Rs. 25,000-** In this case, 8.0% respondents have strongly agreed, 54.0% respondents have agreed, 4.7% respondents were neutral, 22.0% respondents have disagreed and 11.3% respondents have strongly disagreed.

- **Between Rs 25,001 to Rs. 50,000-** In this case, 15.5% respondents have strongly agreed, 60.7% respondents have agreed, 6.5% respondents were neutral, 13.3% respondents have disagreed and 4.0% respondents have strongly disagreed.

- **Between Rs 50,001 to Rs. 75,000-** In this case, 17.9% respondents have strongly agreed, 52.4% respondents have agreed, 5.7% respondents were neutral, 18.4% respondents have disagreed and 5.7% respondents have strongly disagreed.

- **Between Rs 75,001 to Rs. 1,00,000-** In this case, 14.8% respondents have strongly agreed, 53.3% respondents have agreed, 7.5% respondents were neutral, 19.1% respondents have disagreed and 5.2% respondents have strongly disagreed.

- **Above Rs. 1,00,000-** In this case, 21.4% respondents have strongly agreed, 54.5% respondents have agreed, 4.5% respondents were neutral, 17.0% respondents have disagreed and 2.7% respondents have strongly disagreed.

$H_{05.5.2}$: *There is no significant difference between Respondents' Investing Behavior and their Monthly Income regarding variable- All non-vegetarian Products.*

Table 4.105- Chi Square Tests: Difference between Investing Behavior and Monthly Income (All non-vegetarian Products)

Chi-Square Tests			
	Value	df	Asymptotic Significance (2-sided)
Pearson Chi-Square	27.903[a]	16	.032

Findings and Interpretation: As per the Chi Square Tests, Pearson Chi-Square comes out to be significant (p value .032<.05). It means that there is significant difference between respondents' Investing Behavior and their Monthly Income regarding variable- All non-vegetarian Products. Therefore $H_{05.5.2}$ is rejected.

Table 4.106- Crosstab: All Non-Vegetarian Products

| | | | \multicolumn{5}{c}{All Non-Vegetarian Products} | |
			Strongly Disagree	Disagree	Neutral	Agree	Strongly Agree	Total
Monthly Income	Below Rs. 25,000	Count	15	66	21	45	3	150
		% within	10.0%	44.0%	14.0%	30.0%	2.0%	100.0%
	Between Rs 25,001 to Rs. 50,000	Count	39	165	34	75	10	323
		% within	12.1%	51.1%	10.5%	23.2%	3.1%	100.0%
	Between Rs 50,001 to Rs. 75,000	Count	33	104	20	50	5	212
		% within	15.6%	49.1%	9.4%	23.6%	2.4%	100.0%
	Between Rs 75,001 to Rs. 1,00,000	Count	51	193	49	113	33	439
		% within	11.6%	44.0%	11.2%	25.7%	7.5%	100.0%
	Above Rs. 1,00,000.	Count	7	51	15	33	6	112
		% within	6.3%	45.5%	13.4%	29.5%	5.4%	100.0%
Total		Count	145	579	139	316	57	1236
		% within	11.7%	46.8%	11.2%	25.6%	4.6%	100.0%

The above table shows that there are total 1236 respondents (General Public). The Monthly Income wise break-up of these respondents when asked about their about their unwillingness for investing in All Non-Vegetarian Products- is as follows-

- **Below Rs. 25,000-** In this case, 2.0% respondents have strongly agreed, 30.0% respondents have agreed, 14.0% respondents were neutral, 44.0% respondents have disagreed and 10.0% respondents have strongly disagreed.

- **Between Rs 25,001 to Rs. 50,000-** In this case, 3.1% respondents have strongly agreed, 23.2% respondents have agreed, 10.5% respondents were neutral, 51.1% respondents have disagreed and 12.1% respondents have strongly disagreed.

- **Between Rs 50,001 to Rs. 75,000-** In this case, 2.4% respondents have strongly agreed, 23.6% respondents have agreed, 9.4% respondents were neutral, 49.1% respondents have disagreed and 15.6% respondents have strongly disagreed.

- **Between Rs 75,001 to Rs. 1,00,000-** In this case, 7.5% respondents have strongly agreed, 25.7% respondents have agreed, 11.2% respondents were neutral, 44.0% respondents have disagreed and 11.6% respondents have strongly disagreed.

- **Above Rs. 1,00,000-** In this case, 5.4% respondents have strongly agreed, 29.5% respondents have agreed, 13.4% respondents were neutral, 45.5% respondents have disagreed and 6.3% respondents have strongly disagreed.

$H_{05.5.3}$: *There is no significant difference between Respondents' Investing Behavior and their Monthly Income regarding variable- Arms and Ammunition.*

Table 4.107- Chi Square Tests: Difference between Investing Behavior and Monthly Income (Arms and Ammunition)

Chi-Square Tests			
	Value	df	Asymptotic Significance (2-sided)
Pearson Chi-Square	31.604[a]	16	.011

Findings and Interpretation: As per the Chi Square Tests, Pearson Chi-Square comes out to be significant (p value .011<.05). It means that there is significant difference between respondents' Investing Behavior and their Monthly Income regarding variable- Arms and Ammunition. Therefore $H_{05.5.3}$ is rejected.

Table 4.108- Crosstab: Arms and Ammunition

Crosstab								
			Arms and Ammunition					
			Strongly Disagree	Disagree	Neutral	Agree	Strongly Agree	Total
Monthly Income	Below Rs. 25,000	Count	34	84	29	3	0	150
		% within	22.7%	56.0%	19.3%	2.0%	0.0%	100.0%
	Between Rs 25,001 to Rs. 50,000	Count	45	203	64	6	5	323
		% within	13.9%	62.8%	19.8%	1.9%	1.5%	100.0%
	Between Rs 50,001 to Rs. 75,000	Count	42	142	20	7	1	212
		% within	19.8%	67.0%	9.4%	3.3%	0.5%	100.0%

Between Rs 75,001 to Rs. 1,00,000	Count	66	279	66	21	7	439
	% within	15.0%	63.6%	15.0%	4.8%	1.6%	100.0%
Above Rs. 1,00,000.	Count	15	70	21	6	0	112
	% within	13.4%	62.5%	18.8%	5.4%	0.0%	100.0%
Total	Count	202	778	200	43	13	1236
	% within	16.3%	62.9%	16.2%	3.5%	1.1%	100.0%

The above table shows that there are total 1236 respondents (General Public). The Monthly Income wise break-up of these respondents when asked about their unwillingness for investing in Arms and Ammunition- is as follows-

- **Below Rs. 25,000-** In this case, 0.0% respondents have strongly agreed, 2.0% respondents have agreed, 19.3% respondents were neutral, 56.0% respondents have disagreed and 22.7% respondents have strongly disagreed.

- **Between Rs 25,001 to Rs. 50,000-** In this case, 1.5% respondents have strongly agreed, 1.9% respondents have agreed, 19.8% respondents were neutral, 62.8% respondents have disagreed and 13.9% respondents have strongly disagreed.

- **Between Rs 50,001 to Rs. 75,000-** In this case, 0.5% respondents have strongly agreed, 3.3% respondents have agreed, 9.4% respondents were neutral, 67.0% respondents have disagreed and 19.8% respondents have strongly disagreed.

- **Between Rs 75,001 to Rs. 1,00,000-** In this case, 1.6% respondents have strongly agreed, 4.8% respondents have agreed, 15.0% respondents were neutral, 63.6% respondents have disagreed and 15.0% respondents have strongly disagreed.

- **Above Rs. 1,00,000-** In this case, 0.0% respondents have strongly agreed, 5.4% respondents have agreed, 18.8% respondents were neutral, 62.5% respondents have disagreed and 13.4% respondents have strongly disagreed.

$H_{05.5.4}$: *There is no significant difference between Respondents' Investing Behavior and their Monthly Income regarding variable- Non-Environment Friendly Products.*

Table 4.109- Chi Square Tests: Difference between Investing Behavior and Monthly Income (Non-Environment Friendly Products)

Chi-Square Tests			
	Value	df	Asymptotic Significance (2-sided)
Pearson Chi-Square	47.764[a]	16	.000

Findings and Interpretation: As per the Chi Square Tests, Pearson Chi-Square comes out to be significant (p value .000<.05). It means that there is significant difference between respondents' Investing Behavior and their Monthly Income regarding variable- Non-Environment Friendly Products. Therefore $H_{05.5.4}$ is rejected.

Table 4.110- Crosstab: Non-Environment Friendly Products

			Non-Environment Friendly Products					
			Strongly Disagree	Disagree	Neutral	Agree	Strongly Agree	Total
Monthly Income	Below Rs. 25,000	Count	20	43	27	46	14	150
		% within	13.3%	28.7%	18.0%	30.7%	9.3%	100.0%
	Between Rs 25,001 to Rs. 50,000	Count	12	92	55	96	68	323
		% within	3.7%	28.5%	17.0%	29.7%	21.1%	100.0%
	Between Rs 50,001 to Rs. 75,000	Count	13	46	43	51	59	212
		% within	6.1%	21.7%	20.3%	24.1%	27.8%	100.0%
	Between Rs 75,001 to Rs. 1,00,000	Count	20	99	92	126	102	439
		% within	4.6%	22.6%	21.0%	28.7%	23.2%	100.0%
	Above Rs. 1,00,000.	Count	5	18	23	33	33	112
		% within	4.5%	16.1%	20.5%	29.5%	29.5%	100.0%
Total		Count	70	298	240	352	276	1236
		% within	5.7%	24.1%	19.4%	28.5%	22.3%	100.0%

The above table shows that there are total 1236 respondents (General Public). The Monthly Income wise break-up of these respondents when asked about their unwillingness for investing in Non-Environment Friendly Products- is as follows-

- **Below Rs. 25,000-** In this case, 9.3% respondents have strongly agreed, 30.7% respondents have agreed, 18.0% respondents were neutral, 28.7% respondents have disagreed and 13.3% respondents have strongly disagreed.

- **Between Rs 25,001 to Rs. 50,000-** In this case, 21.1% respondents have strongly agreed, 29.7% respondents have agreed, 17.0% respondents were neutral, 28.5% respondents have disagreed and 3.7% respondents have strongly disagreed.

- **Between Rs 50,001 to Rs. 75,000-** In this case, 27.8% respondents have strongly agreed, 24.1% respondents have agreed, 20.3% respondents were neutral, 21.7% respondents have disagreed and 6.1% respondents have strongly disagreed.

- **Between Rs 75,001 to Rs. 1,00,000-** In this case, 23.2% respondents have strongly agreed, 28.7% respondents have agreed, 21.0% respondents were neutral, 22.6% respondents have disagreed and 4.6% respondents have strongly disagreed.

- **Above Rs. 1,00,000-** In this case, 29.5% respondents have strongly agreed, 29.5% respondents have agreed, 20.5% respondents were neutral, 16.1% respondents have disagreed and 4.5% respondents have strongly disagreed.

$H_{05.5.5}$: *There is no significant difference between Respondents' Investing Behavior and their Monthly Income regarding variable- Products that involves animal cruelty.*

Table 4.111- Chi Square Tests: Difference between Investing Behavior and Monthly Income (Products that involves animal cruelty)

Chi-Square Tests			
	Value	df	Asymptotic Significance (2-sided)
Pearson Chi-Square	23.701[a]	8	.003

Findings and Interpretation: As per the Chi Square Tests, Pearson Chi-Square comes out to be significant (p value .003<.05). It means that there is significant difference between consumers' Investing Behavior and their Monthly Income regarding variable- Products that involves Animal Cruelty. Therefore $H_{05.5.5}$ is rejected.

Table 4.112- Crosstab: Products that involves Animal Cruelty

Crosstab						
			Products that involves Animal Cruelty			
			Neutral	Agree	Strongly Agree	Total
Monthly Income	Below Rs. 25,000	Count	26	88	36	150
		% within	17.3%	58.7%	24.0%	100.0%
	Between Rs 25,001 to Rs. 50,000	Count	24	191	108	323
		% within	7.4%	59.1%	33.4%	100.0%
	Between Rs 50,001 to Rs. 75,000	Count	25	105	82	212
		% within	11.8%	49.5%	38.7%	100.0%

Between Rs 75,001 to Rs. 1,00,000	Count	49	248	142	439
	% within	11.2%	56.5%	32.3%	100.0%
Above Rs. 1,00,000.	Count	8	55	49	112
	% within	7.1%	49.1%	43.8%	100.0%
Total	Count	132	687	417	1236
	% within	10.7%	55.6%	33.7%	100.0%

The above table shows that there are total 1236 respondents (General Public). The monthly income wise break-up of these respondents when asked about their unwillingness for investing in Products that involves Animal Cruelty- is as follows-

- **Below Rs. 25,000-** In this case, 24.0% respondents have strongly agreed, 58.7% respondents have agreed, and 17.3% respondents were neutral.

- **Between Rs 25,001 to Rs. 50,000-** In this case, 33.4% respondents have strongly agreed, 59.1% respondents have agreed, and 7.4% respondents were neutral.

- **Between Rs 50,001 to Rs. 75,000-** In this case, 38.7% respondents have strongly agreed, 49.5% respondents have agreed, and 11.8 respondents were neutral.

- **Between Rs 75,001 to Rs. 1,00,000-** In this case, 32.3% respondents have strongly agreed, 56.5% respondents have agreed, and 11.2% respondents were neutral.

- **Above Rs. 1,00,000-** In this case, 43.8% respondents have strongly agreed, 49.1% respondents have agreed, and 7.1% respondents were neutral.

CHAPTER 5: FINDINGS, CONCLUSION AND RECOMMENDATIONS

The present study gives a comprehensive exploration and analysis of a specific research question within a particular field of study. Through an exhaustive review of the literature, meticulous data collection, and rigorous analysis, the researcher not only addresses the identified research gap but also provides a foundation for future scholarship and practical applications.

5.1 Findings of the Study

The most important factors of Awareness of **IFB** for General Public were related to interest free loans, trade with mark up and special type of trading agreement. Whereas in case of Bank Officials, the most important factors of Awareness of IFB were related to interest free loans, special type of trading agreement, leasing and sales contracts.

The most important factors of Acceptability of **IFB** for General Public were related to eliminating contract ambiguity and involvement in only real economic transactions having a tangible asset, prohibiting morally and socially harmful activities, preserving equity principles are preserved and profit and loss sharing. Whereas in case of Bank Officials, the most important factors of Acceptability of **IFB** were related to freedom from all forms of exploitations and justice between the financer and the entrepreneur, profit and loss sharing and no fixed rate of return.

The most important factors of Business potential of **IFB** for General Public were related to the transactions that are backed by a tangible asset, emphasis on social activities, principle of prohibition of excessive risk and potential benefit to depositors as well as the bank. Whereas in case of Bank Officials, the most important factors of Business potential of **IFB** were related to the large customer base and possibility of increase in Business Potential of **IFB**. Along with these factors, development of IFB System for all citizens and incorporation of regulatory body, were also the most important factors of Business potential of **IFB** for Bank Officials.

5.1.1 Hypotheses wise Findings

Hypotheses	Supported/ Not Supported
Research Objective 1: To test the Awareness Level of Respondents regarding Interest Free Banking.	
$H_{1.1}$: There is a significant difference between Male and Female Respondents among General Public regarding Awareness Level of IFB.	**Supported**
$H_{1.2}$: There is a significant difference between Government Bank and Private Bank Respondents among Bank Officials regarding Awareness Level of IFB.	**Not Supported**
Research Objective 2: To identify whether current Banks (Private as well as Govt.) will be ready to introduce Interest Free Banking or not if investors are ready to adopt it.	
$H_{2.1}$: There is a significant impact of Awareness Level on the Acceptability Level of IFB from the perspective of General Public.	**Not Supported**
$H_{2.2}$: There is a significant impact of Awareness Level on the Acceptability Level of IFB from the perspective of Bank Officials.	**Supported**
$H_{2.3}$: There is a significant difference between Male and Female Respondents among General Public regarding Acceptability Level of IFB.	**Supported**
$H_{2.4}$: There is a significant difference between Government Bank and Private Bank Respondents among Bank Officials regarding Acceptability Level of IFB.	**Not Supported**
Research Objective 3: To explore the Business Potential of Interest Free Banking in India.	
$H_{3.1}$: There is a significant impact of Awareness Level on Business Potential of IFB from the perspective of General Public.	**Supported**
$H_{3.2}$: There is a significant impact of Awareness Level on Business Potential of IFB from the perspective of Bank Officials.	**Not Supported**
$H_{3.3}$: There is a significant impact of Acceptability Level on Business Potential of IFB from the perspective of General Public.	**Supported**
$H_{3.4}$: There is a significant impact of Acceptability Level on Business Potential of IFB from the perspective of Bank officials.	**Supported**
$H_{3.5}$: There is a significant difference between Male and Female Respondents among General Public regarding Business Potential of IFB.	**Not Supported**
$H_{3.6}$: There is a significant difference between Government Bank and Private Bank Respondents among Bank Officials regarding Business Potential of IFB.	**Not Supported**
Research Objective 4: To identify the impact of Religion on Investing Behavior of Respondents.	

H$_{4.1}$: There is a significant difference between Investing Behavior of Respondents and their Religions.	
H$_{4.1.1}$: There is a significant difference between Respondents' Investing Behavior and their Religion regarding variable that emphasizes on social activities.	**Supported**
H$_{4.1.2}$: There is a significant difference between Respondents' Investing Behavior and their Religion regarding variable that works on the principle of Prohibition of excessive risk/uncertainty.	**Supported**
H$_{4.1.3}$: There is a significant difference between Respondents' Investing Behavior and their Religion regarding variable that only allows the transactions that are backed by a tangible asset.	**Supported**
H$_{4.1.4}$: There is a significant difference between Respondents' Investing Behavior and their Religion regarding variable that does not approve financing of alcohol.	**Supported**
H$_{4.1.5}$: There is a significant difference between Respondents' Investing Behavior and their Religion regarding variable that does not approve financing of pork.	**Supported**
H$_{4.1.6}$: There is a significant difference between Respondents' Investing Behavior and their Religion regarding variable that does not approve financing of ammunitions.	**Supported**
Research Objective 5: To identify the influence of demographic variables (Age, Gender, Educational Qualifications, Occupation and Monthly Income) on Investing Behavior of Respondents.	
H$_5$: There is a significant difference between Respondents' Investing Behavior and their demographic variables (Age, Gender, Education, Occupation and Monthly Income).	
H$_{5.1}$: There is a significant difference between Respondents' Investing Behavior and their Age.	
H$_{5.1.1}$: There is a significant difference between Respondents' Investing Behavior and their Age regarding variable-Tobacco/Alcohol products.	**Supported**
H$_{5.1.2}$: There is a significant difference between Respondents' Investing Behavior and their Age regarding variable- All Non-Vegetarian Products.	**Supported**
H$_{5.1.3}$: There is a significant difference between Respondents' Investing Behavior and their Age regarding variable- Arms and Ammunition.	**Not Supported**
H$_{5.1.4}$: There is a significant difference between Respondents' Investing Behavior and their Age regarding variable- Non-Environment Friendly Products.	**Supported**
H$_{5.1.5}$: There is a significant difference between Respondents' Investing Behavior and their Age regarding variable- Products that involves animal cruelty.	**Supported**

144

$H_{5.2}$: There is a significant difference between Respondents' Investing Behavior and their Gender.	
$H_{5.2.1}$: There is a significant difference between Respondents' Investing Behavior and their Gender regarding variable- Tobacco/Alcohol products.	**Not Supported**
$H_{5.2.2}$: There is a significant difference between Respondents' Investing Behavior and their Gender regarding variable- All non-vegetarian Products.	**Not Supported**
$H_{5.2.3}$: There is a significant difference between Respondents' Investing Behavior and their Gender regarding variable- Arms and Ammunition.	**Not Supported**
$H_{5.2.4}$: There is a significant difference between Respondents' Investing Behavior and their Gender regarding variable- Non-Environment Friendly Products.	**Not Supported**
$H_{5.2.5}$: There is a significant difference between Respondents' Investing Behavior and their Gender regarding variable- Products that involves Animal Cruelty.	**Not Supported**
$H_{5.3}$: There is a significant difference between Respondents' Investing Behavior and their Educational Qualifications.	
$H_{5.3.1}$: There is a significant difference between Respondents' Investing Behavior and their Educational Qualifications regarding variable- Tobacco/Alcohol products.	**Supported**
$H_{5.3.2}$: There is a significant difference between Respondents' Investing Behavior and their Educational Qualifications regarding variable- All non-vegetarian Products.	**Not Supported**
$H_{5.3.3}$: There is a significant difference between Respondents' Investing Behavior and their Educational Qualifications regarding variable- Arms and Ammunition.	**Not Supported**
$H_{5.3.4}$: There is a significant difference between Respondents' Investing Behavior and their Educational Qualifications regarding variable- Non-Environment Friendly Products.	**Not Supported**
$H_{5.3.5}$: There is a significant difference between Respondents' Investing Behavior and their Educational Qualifications regarding variable- Products that involves animal cruelty.	**Not Supported**
$H_{5.4}$: There is a significant difference between Respondents' Investing Behavior and their Occupation.	
$H_{5.4.1}$: There is a significant difference between Respondents' Investing Behavior and their Occupation regarding variable- Tobacco/Alcohol products.	**Supported**
$H_{5.4.2}$: There is a significant difference between Respondents' Investing Behavior and their Occupation regarding variable- All non-vegetarian Products.	**Supported**
$H_{5.4.3}$: There is a significant difference between Respondents'	**Supported**

Investing Behavior and their Occupation regarding variable- Arms and Ammunition.	
$H_{5.4.4}$: There is a significant difference between Respondents' Investing Behavior and their Occupation regarding variable- Non-Environment Friendly Products.	**Supported**
$H_{5.4.5}$: There is a significant difference between Respondents' Investing Behavior and their Occupation regarding variable- Products that involves animal cruelty.	**Supported**
$H_{5.5}$: There is a significant difference between Respondents' Investing Behavior and their Monthly Income.	
$H_{5.5.1}$: There is a significant difference between Respondents' Investing Behavior and their Monthly Income regarding variable- Tobacco/Alcohol products.	**Supported**
$H_{5.5.2}$: There is a significant difference between Respondents' Investing Behavior and their Monthly Income regarding variable- All non-vegetarian Products.	**Supported**
$H_{5.5.3}$: There is a significant difference between Respondents' Investing Behavior and their Monthly Income regarding variable- Arms and Ammunition.	**Supported**
$H_{5.5.4}$: There is a significant difference between Respondents' Investing Behavior and their Monthly Income regarding variable- Non-Environment Friendly Products.	**Supported**
$H_{5.5.5}$: There is a significant difference between Respondents' Investing Behavior and their Monthly Income regarding variable- Products that involves animal cruelty.	**Supported**

5.2 Discussion and Conclusion

In India, the ideas, operations, and practices of Conventional Banking System and **IFB** widely known as "Islamic Banking", are very different. Interest-based lending and borrowing are the cornerstones on which Conventional Banks base their operations. Interest is assessed and paid on loans and deposits, respectively. These banks prioritize making money for their shareholders. In contrast, **IFB** adheres to *Shariah* norms, which forbid the collection or payment of interest (***Riba***). Rather, it places a strong emphasis on profit and loss sharing (PLS) and adherence to moral and ethical standards.

The main way to make money in the Conventional Banking system is through interest. In order to make money, banks charge interest on loans that is more than the cost of borrowing. Interest on loans or deposits is not assessed or paid by interest-free institutions. Instead, they

146

participate in fee-based or profit-sharing agreements. Through partnerships (*Mudarabah*) or joint ventures (*Musharakah*), they might offer funding.

Conventional banks make investments in a variety of fields, including business, real estate, and finance. They base their investment choices on profitability and risk factors. Islamic banks follow moral standards for investing. They stay away from industries like gambling, drinking, smoking, and other things that are deemed *Haram* (prohibited) by Islamic law. They focus their investments on *Shariah*-compliant industries like trade, manufacturing, and real estate.

In conventional banking, the borrower shoulders the majority of the risk, leading banks to mitigate their risk exposure by imposing interest charges on loans. In contrast, **IFB** places a significant emphasis on the joint sharing of risks between the bank and the borrower. In profit-sharing agreements, both parties mutually participate in gains and losses. This approach encourages more prudent lending practices and fosters a closer alignment of interests between the bank and the borrower.

Loans, mortgages, credit cards, savings accounts, and investment services are just a few of the numerous goods and services that Conventional banks provide. These goods are made to meet the various requirements of people, organisations, and institutions. Similar products are offered by **IFB**, however their emphasis is on *Shariah* compliance. For instance, they offer Islamic financing solutions such as *Murabahah* (cost-plus financing), *Ijarah* (lease), and *Takaful* (Islamic insurance) in place of conventional interest-bearing loans.

The present study endeavors to comprehend the potentiality of adopting **IFB** in India. Prior to assessing the business potential of **IFB** in the country, the researcher undertook an exploration of the awareness levels regarding the operations and services of the **IFB** system. Subsequently, the study delves into analyzing the acceptability level of such a system in India. A noteworthy aspect of this research lies in its exploration of the perceptions of both the General Public and Bank Officials concerning the key elements of the business potential of a novel banking system. This system markedly differs from the fundamental conventional banking system in India. The investigation aims to shed light on the feasibility and receptivity of **IFB** within the Indian context. The researcher considered to study the perception of both the General Public and Bank Officials while exploring the potential of a new banking system because both are at the two ends where General Public is at the receiving end by being a customer so it is important to understand that whether they will accept a new banking system or not. On the other hand, the opinion of Bank Officials is also important because they will be at the service provider's desk.

Therefore, the present study on the topic- **"Business Potential of Interest Free Banking in India: A Study with Special Reference to Uttar Pradesh"** is an attempt of the researcher to study in detail the business potential of **IFB** in India by focusing on the awareness level, acceptability level and business potential and the inter play of these three dimensions. This study is exploratory and descriptive in design and is primary data based with a total **1236** General Public and **436** Bank Officials from fives selected cities (Kanpur, Prayagraj, Lucknow, Azamgarh, Mau) of Uttar Pradesh. The results of the different dimensions of the study are discussed and concluded below-

❖ **Awareness of Interest Free Banking**

On exploring the most important factors of awareness **of IFB** system and Services, from the perspective of the General Public, the results revealed that **78%** people were aware of the basic facts surrounding **IFB**. The public comprehension of **IFB** was rooted in an understanding of its foundations in Islamic finance principles, particularly the prohibition of charging or paying interest (***Riba***). Instead, the system is based on profit and loss sharing, emphasizing ethical and socially responsible investments. This suggests that the core features and guiding principles of **IFB** were transparent and well-grasped by the General Public.

On the other hand, **63%** Bank Officials demonstrated awareness regarding the operations and services of **IFB**. They were knowledgeable about specific aspects such as special trading agreements, leasing contracts, and sales contracts that are associated with this banking system. Their awareness extended beyond the basic principles and encompassed the practical aspects of **IFB**.

Overall, the findings suggest that both the General Public and Bank Officials possess a certain level of awareness regarding **IFB** system and its services. Despite **IFB** not being operational in India, people have familiarity with its working and basic terms. This awareness level is crucial for understanding the potentiality of **IFB** and assessing its feasibility in the Indian context.

These findings have implications for policymakers, financial institutions, and stakeholders in the banking sector. They provide insights into the existing knowledge base among the

General Public and Bank Officials regarding **IFB**. This awareness can serve as a foundation for future initiatives and educational campaigns aimed at promoting **IFB** and increasing its acceptance.

Further research could delve deeper into the specific areas of awareness and knowledge gaps among the General Public and Bank Officials. This would facilitate the development of targeted strategies to enhance understanding and familiarity with **IFB**, ultimately contributing to its potential adoption and growth in India.

❖ **Acceptability of Interest Free Banking**

The researcher endeavored to comprehend the factors influencing the acceptance of **IFB** among the General Public and Bank Officials. From the perspective of the General Public, the appeal of IFB lies in its ability to eliminate contract ambiguity and exclusively involve real economic transactions backed by tangible assets. In this banking system, activities deemed morally and socially harmful are prohibited. Furthermore, the General Public showed the interest into IFB due to the preservation of participation and equity principles.

While from the perspective of Bank Official, the **IFB** system was found acceptable to them based on the factors like freedom from all forms of exploitations and justice between the financer and the entrepreneur. Risk of loss and variability of profits must be faced to get the returns (profit and loss sharing) and lastly no fixed rate of return on deposits nor is any interest charged on loans.

It can be deduced from the results that based on the above factors General Public and Bank Officials can accept the **IFB** but there is still a need to reach to the unanimous consensus on the acceptability factors of such banking system before operating it.

The future of **IFB** commonly referred to as **IFB** or *Shariah*-compliant banking, in India it is dependent on a number of variables. While **IFB** has become more popular in a number of nations with a plurality of Muslims, India's development has been rather gradual for a variety of reasons. Nevertheless, there are still chances for the country to pursue **IFB**.

IFB adheres to the ethical and responsible banking concepts, which are popularising worldwide. A rising number of people, including non-Muslims, are calling for alternative banking models that uphold moral principles. The Reserve Bank of India (RBI), has expressed some interest in investigating the potential of **IFB**. The RBI established an interdepartmental panel in 2016 to investigate whether **IFB** might be implemented in India. The group's proposals had showed that they were aware of the possibility of **IFB** in the nation, even though they have not yet been put into practice.

For marginalised communities that are hesitant to interact with conventional banking due to religious convictions or worries about interest-based transactions, **IFB** may be a way to promote financial inclusion. The banking industry can serve these underserved sectors by providing *Shariah*-compliant financial solutions, such as interest-free loans. The advent of **IFB** could help the Indian banking industries to diversify, giving customers additional choices and competition. The banking sector's overall efficiency may increase as a result of this diversified potential to spur innovation. Despite these opportunities, there are still issues that must be resolved for **IFB** to be successfully implemented in India.

❖ Business Potential of Interest Free Banking

The study aimed to identify the most important factors related to the business potential of **IFB** and the religious aspects associated with it, from the perspective of the General Public and Bank Officials. From the perspective of the General Public, the results revealed that the most significant factors contributing to the business potential of **IFB** and its religious aspects are freedom from all forms of exploitations and the presence of justice between the financer and the entrepreneur.

On the other hand, Bank Officials expressed their acceptance of the **IFB** system based on their belief that the customer base is sufficiently large to initiate such a banking system in India. They recognized its business potential and expressed optimism that the customer base for **IFB** could grow over time, making it feasible to develop it across the country. Furthermore, Bank Officials emphasized the importance of having a specific regulatory body to govern the operations of the **IFB** system.

The present study provides valuable insights into the perceptions and considerations of both the General Public and Bank Officials regarding the business potential and religious aspects of **IFB**. They highlight the significance of principles such as fairness, risk-sharing, and the absence of exploitative practices in shaping the acceptability and growth potential of **IFB**.

It is also recommended that policymakers and banking institutions should focus on promoting the principles of justice and fairness, as well as effective risk-sharing mechanisms, in order to enhance the business potential and religious aspects of **IFB**. Establishing a dedicated regulatory body could also help in providing a supportive and well-governed framework for the development and expansion of the **IFB** system in India. Further research could explore additional factors and perspectives related to the business potential and religious aspects of **IFB**, providing a more comprehensive understanding of its viability and implications in the banking sector.

❖ **Impact of Awareness Level on Acceptability Level**

After exploring the most important factors of awareness and acceptability of **IFB** in India, the present research moved further to know the influence of the awareness on the acceptability of **IFB** system in India from the perspective of both the general public and the Bank Officials.

In case of General Public, not enough evidence found to conclude that there is a significant relationship between awareness and acceptability in the context under investigation. This finding implies that other factors or variables may play a more influential role in shaping the acceptability level among the General Public in this particular scenario.

It was found that awareness of **IFB** system was influencing its acceptability positively from the viewpoint of Bank Officials. It was revealed that the positive impact was significant in case of Bank Officials. It can be deduced from the findings that awareness of General Public is not that instrumental in accepting a new banking system but what matters more is the awareness of Bank Officials that will significantly impact that whether they are willing to accept a new system of banking or not.

❖ **Impact of Acceptability Level on Business Potential**

The fact that there is a positive and significant correlation between the acceptance of the **IFB** system and its commercial viability among both the General Public and Bank Officials is another noteworthy finding from this study. According to the findings, the business potential for this banking model is stronger when the **IFB** system is more widely accepted.

This result is consistent with the intuitive perception that a company's potential is directly related to how well it is received by its target market. If people and banking professionals are more willing to accept and embrace this alternative banking model in the case of the **IFB** system, it suggests a bigger potential for success and expansion.

The findings highlight how important it is to raise knowledge of and cultivate a favourable view of the **IFB** system in order to promote its acceptance and hence increase its commercial potential. Marketing, education, and awareness initiatives that clear up misconceptions highlight the advantages, and foster trust in this banking system may help it gain wider adoption and subsequently increase its commercial potential.

Understanding the significance of acceptance and its impact on business potential is vital for policymakers, financial institutions, and players in the **IFB** industry. They can encourage the expansion and viability of the **IFB** system by creating a supportive environment and removing any obstacles to acceptance.

The study reflected the connection between acceptability and commercial viability within the context of the **IFB** system. This research has significant implications in strategic planning, marketing, and policy-making for **IFB**, aiming to improve acceptance and maximize its financial potential.

❖ **General Public's Religion, Gender, Age, Occupation, Educational Qualification and their Investing Behavior**

Additionally, the researcher was interested in learning how respondents' demographic characteristics affected their investment behavior. The results showed that religion differentiated investing choices, which is consistent with the individuals' adherence to their respective religious tenets and principles. For instance, some religions forbid investing in certain industries, such as the Tobacco or Alcohol industries.

On the other hand, it was not discovered that gender had a substantial impact on investment behavior. This shows that other factors rather than gender largely influence investing decisions. Occupation has been found to have a major impact on investment behavior. This suggests that people's career choices can affect their investing choices, possibly as a result of different financial resources, risk tolerances, or exposure to investment options.

Respondents under the present study were typically unwilling to spend money on weapons and ammunition, tobacco/alcohol, non-vegetarian, non-environment friendly products and products involving animal cruelty, however, showed substantial disparities in investment decisions. Although, different age groups may have different beliefs and attitudes that influence how they make investments.

An important difference was found in the decision to invest in tobacco and alcohol products according to the link between educational background and investment behavior. This demonstrates how schooling shapes people's attitudes and preferences towards this kind of activities. However, Education level did not have a substantial impact on investment choices in relation to non-vegetarian products, weapons and ammunition, unfriendly items to the environment, and goods that include animal cruelty.

These findings offer general understanding of the relationship between demographic characteristics and investment behavior. It draws attention to the role that factors like religion, profession, age and education play in influencing people's choices to invest in particular markets or goods. These results can help investors, financial advisors, and policymakers better understand the variables that affect investment behavior and adjust their plans.

5.3 Suggestions

IFB has become well-known throughout the world for its commitment to socially responsible investing, risk sharing, and economic fairness. India has the chance to diversify its financial industry, meet the needs of a sizable Muslim population and include others too, and draw foreign investment by embracing **IFB**. Following suggestions can be set forth in line with the discussion and conclusion detailed above-

- To familiarise the General Public, including people, companies, and financial institutions, with the ideas and advantages of **IFB**, a thorough awareness campaign is necessary. This can be accomplished through educational programmes, seminars and workshops led by professionals in Islamic finance.
- Collaboration with media outlets and educational institutions can aid in the dissemination of truthful information about **IFB**.
- To guarantee the integrity and authenticity of **IFB** practices, it is essential to establish a strong and independent *Shariah* compliance process. A *Shariah* **Board** made up of prominent scholars of Islamic finance and jurisprudence should make up the system. They would be in charge of ensuring that **IFB** followed *Shariah* guidelines and offering the appropriate direction.
- A variety of financial solutions are available from **IFB** that are based on concepts including profit-sharing (*Mudarabah*), cost-plus financing (*Murabahah*), and leasing (*Ijarah*).

- In-depth analysis and professional collaboration should be performed to build and create cutting-edge Islamic financial solutions that meet the different needs of Indian citizens and companies.

- Collaboration between reputable Islamic financial institutions from other nations and Indian banks can promote capacity building, knowledge transfer, and technology sharing. This partnership will improve Indian banks' capacity to provide **IFB** and enable a seamless transition.

- To maintain a level playing field for **IFB** and conventional banking and prevent any discriminatory practices, tax rules should also be examined.

- Building trust and acceptance among various communities in India requires developing social integration and interfaith discourse. Discussing the advantages of **IFB** with community groups, religious leaders, and civil society can help dispel myths and foster an atmosphere of respect and understanding.

- The advancement of new financial instruments and solutions might result promoting research and development in the area of Islamic finance.

- Studies on the socioeconomic effects of **IFB** in India can be advanced by collaboration with academic institutions and research centres, assuring the use of evidence in decision-making.

- **IFB** in India has a variety of difficulties that must be addressed with caution and forethought. To accommodate the distinctive principles and requirements of **IFB**, the regulatory structure and legal framework must be reinforced. The industry will expand and investor confidence will increase if laws are clear and consistent.

- Educating Indians about **IFB** and removing their misconceptions about it is another important task. Building confidence and fostering greater acceptance will be made easier by educating the public about the tenets and advantages of Islamic financing.

- Furthermore, it is critical to create a strong infrastructure and broaden the availability of **IFB** services and products throughout the nation. More people and companies will choose Islamic financial solutions if accessibility and ease are improved.

Among the Indian populace, including potential customers and policymakers, **IFB** is not generally known about or understood. In order to close this knowledge gap and encourage adoption of alternative banking methods, education and awareness initiatives are essential. For its implementation to be successful, a strong infrastructure and expertise in **IFB** procedures must be developed. It will take a lot of money and work to build the necessary infrastructure, educate specialists, and develop a supporting ecosystem. Political opposition to **IFB** could arise for ideological or cultural reasons. It can be difficult to get over this opposition and create consensus among different parties. India can successfully introduce **IFB** and take use of the enormous potential of ethical and inclusive finance by putting the above-mentioned suggestions into practise. **IFB** has proven to be resilient in international markets and may make a significant contribution to India's financial industry while fostering financial inclusion and socioeconomic growth.

5.4 Limitations

The goal of the current study was to thoroughly analyse the commercial possibilities of **IFB** in India, with an emphasis on Uttar Pradesh. To develop a comprehensive grasp of the topic, the viewpoints of both the General Public and Bank Officials were taken into account. Even though the study significantly added to the body of knowledge, there are still some limitations that need to be acknowledged.

- The use of data gathered at a specific point in time is one of the main limitations of this study. Longitudinal research, which can offer insights into the dynamics and changes in the commercial potential of **IFB** over time, was not taken into account in the study. Researchers could go further to study challenge, identify any changing trends, and provide a more comprehensive view of the topic by conducting longitudinal studies.

- The study also concentrated particularly on the Indian state of Uttar Pradesh. This geographic scope allows for in-depth study and contextual understanding, but it might restrict how broadly the results can be applied to other states or regions of the nation. The socioeconomic conditions, cultural norms, and levels of knowledge and acceptability of **IFB** may change from state to state, which may have an impact on the business potential in different ways. Therefore, future studies should think about broadening their focus to cover a wider range of Indian locations.

- Additionally, the study mostly used survey data and self-report measures, which can have biases and limits. The accuracy and dependability of the results may be impacted by the social desirability bias or other individual opinions that may have an impact on participant responses. Future research should take into account using mixed-methods approaches, integrating qualitative interviews or observations to provide a more thorough knowledge of the business possibilities of **IFB** in order to lessen this limitation.

Future research should overcome the constraints indicated above in order to expand on the findings of this study and further enhance the understanding of the commercial possibilities of **IFB**. Researchers can acquire a deeper understanding of the dynamics, variables, and implications related to **IFB** in India by using mixed-methods approaches, longitudinal research designs, and broadening the geographic reach.

5.5 Future Scope

There are many prospects for additional investigation and research in the topic of **IFB** in India, which has a very broad future scope of study.

- Additionally, solving the complex problems encountered by bankers in the **IFB** industry might greatly benefit from interdisciplinary collaborations. Researchers can investigate multidisciplinary approaches to problem-solving by bringing together professionals from several domains such as finance, technology, law, and ethics. This cooperative effort can help with the creation of creative approaches and plans to get around problems and support the expansion of **IFB** in India.

- Another direction for future research is to broaden the geographic scope of the study. While the current study concentrated on Uttar Pradesh, performing comparable research in other Indian states or cities would give a more comprehensive view of the awareness, acceptability, and commercial viability of **IFB**. Researchers can gain a deeper knowledge of the factors driving **IFB** across the nation by including a wide range of regions with different socioeconomic, cultural, and financial literacy levels.

- Future studies might also explore the potential benefits and drawbacks of **IFB** system. A thorough evaluation of viability of **IFB** and its influence on the Indian banking industry would involve examining the possible advantages, such as financial inclusion, ethical investments, and risk-sharing systems, as well as the difficulties and issues related to it. This analysis can assist financial institutions, governments, and regulators in developing plans of action to take advantage of **IFB** and handle any potential downsides.

- Last but not least, a key subject for future research is examining the role of the government in the expansion and development of the banking sector in India.

Examining the government's initiatives, laws, and rules that enable **IFB** can provide insight into the larger context in which this financial system functions. A thorough comprehension of the industry and its potential for expansion would benefit from knowledge of the government's role in encouraging financial inclusion, providing regulatory oversight, and building an atmosphere that is suitable to **IFB**.

In a nutshell, there is a huge future research potential in the area of **IFB** in India. Researchers can investigate emerging technology, interdisciplinary partnerships, broader geographic coverage, potential benefits and drawbacks, and the function of the government. These research fields have the potential to offer insightful information and support the expansion and development of **IFB** in India, ultimately encouraging inclusive financial practices.

BIBLIOGRAPHY

- AAOIFI (1999). Accounting, Auditing and Governance Standards for Islamic Financial Institutions. Manamah, AAOIFI.

- Abdul-Majid, M., Saal, D. S., and Battisti, G. (2009), The impact of Islamic banking on the cost efficiency and productivity change of Malaysian commercial banks. Applied Economics, 1(22).

- Abdul-Majid, M., Saal, D. S., and Battisti, G. (2010), Efficiency in Islamic and conventional banking: An international comparison. Journal of Productivity Analysis, 34(1), 25–43.

- Abratt, R. and Russel, J. (1999), Relationship marketing in private banking in South Africa. International Journal of Bank Marketing, 17(1):5-19.

- Ahangar, G., Padder, M., & Ganie, A. (2013). Islamic Banking and its scope in India. International Journal of Commerce, Business and Management, 266-269.

- AI-Suwailem, S. (2000). "Towards an Objective Measure of Gharar in Exchange". Islamic Economic Studies 7(1&2): pp.61-102.

- Akhatova, M., Zainal, M.P. and Ibrahim, M.H., (2016), Banking models and monetary transmission mechanisms in Malaysia: Are Islamic banks different? The Economic Society of Australia. Economic Papers 35 (June (2)), 169–183.

- Al Mannai, M., and Ahmed, H., 2018, Exploring the Workings of Shari'ah Supervisory Board in Islamic Finance: A Perspective of Shari'ah Scholars from GCC, The Quarterly Review of Economics and Finance.

- Ali, M., and Azmi, W., (2016), Religion in the Boardroom and Its Impact on Islamic Banks' Performance. Review of Financial Economics, 31, 83–88.

- Ali, S.N. 1993. Information on Islamic banking and economics as represented by selected databases. International Journal of Information Management, 13:205-219.

- Alkhamees, A., (2013), The Impact of Shari'ah Governance Practices on Shari'ah Compliance in Contemporary Islamic Finance. Journal of Banking Regulation, 14(2), 134–163.

- Allan, AJ, Randy, LJ, 2005, Writing the Winning Thesis or Dissertation. A Step-by-Step Guide, Corwin Press, California.

- Al-Omar, F. and Abdel-Haq, M. (1996), Islamic banking: theory, practice and challenges (1st Ed.) London: Zed Books.

➢ Amin, H. (2008), Choice criteria for Islamic home financing empirical investigation among Malaysian bank customers. International Journal of Housing Markets and Analysis, 1(3):256-274.

➢ Ansari A and Tariq H (2016), Interest Free Banking in the Contemporary Banking System, RJCBS: Volume: 05, Number: 04.

➢ Anuar, K., Mohamad, S., and Shah, M. E. (2014), Are deposit and investment accounts in Islamic Banks in Malaysia interest free? JKAU: Islamic Economics, 27(2), 27e55.

➢ Ariss, R. T. (2010), Competitive conditions in Islamic and conventional banking: A global perspective. Review of Financial Economics, 19(3), 101–108.

➢ Arshad, N.C., Zakaria, R.H. and Mohamed, A.A.S., (2015), An empirical assessment of the displaced commercial risk in Malaysian Islamic banking institutions: bank profitability model evidence. Journal of Islamic Banking and Finance (April–June), 78–94.

➢ Ayub, M., 2002. Islamic Banking and Finance: Theory and Practice. State Bank of Pakistan, Karachi, Pakistan.

➢ Babbie, (1998). Survey Research Methods (2nded.). Belmont: Wadsworth. Ch. 18.

➢ Bacha, O. (2004). Dual banking systems and interest rate risk for Islamic banks. The Journal of Accounting, Commerce and Finance e Islamic Perspective, 1(8), 1e42.

➢ Banking Regulation Act.1949 (Act 10 of 1949).

➢ Ba-Owaidan, M. (1994). The Contribution of Accounting Information to Investor Decisions in the Saudi Stock Market. Hull, University of Hull. Ph.D.

➢ Barclay, D. W. (1991). Interdepartmental Conflict in Organizational Buying: The Impact of the Organizational Context. Journal of Marketing Research, 28(2), 145-159.

➢ Bashir, A. H. M. (1999), Risk and profitability measures in Islamic banks: The case of two Sudanese banks. Islamic Economic Studies, 2, 1–24.

➢ Beck, T., A. Demirgüç-Kunt and O. Merrouche, (2013), "Islamic vs. Conventional Banking Business Model, Efficiency and Stability", Journal of Banking and Finance No. 37 Vol. 2, pp. 433–47.

➢ Birben B, (2013), Developments of new interest – free banking instruments in Turkish participation banking sector.

➢ Björklund, M., & Paulsson, U., 2003. Seminarieboken—att skriva, presentera och opponera. Lund: Student litteratur.

➢ Blackson, C., Chen, M.S.J. and Spears. (2007), Determinants of banks selection in USA, Taiwan & Ghana, International Journal of Bank Marketing, 25(7):469-489.

➢ Brian K, (2011), Case studies in Islamic Banking and finance.

➢ Brown RB, (2006), Doing Your Dissertation in Business and Management: The Reality of Research and Writing, Sage Publications.

➢ Burns, A.C. and R.F. Bush, 2003. Marketing Research: Online Research Application. 4th Ed., Prentice Hall, New Jersey, pp: 672.

➢ Cevik, S., and Charap, J. (2011), The behavior of conventional and Islamic Bank Deposit returns in Malaysia and Turkey. IMF Working Paper, WP/11/156.

➢ Chapra, I. U., Ahmed, A., Rehan, R., and Hussain, F. (2018), Consumer's preference and awareness: Comparative analysis between conventional and Islamic Ijarah auto financing in Pakistan. Al-Iqtishad Journal of Islamic Economics, 10(2), 389–402.

➢ Chapra, M.U., and Ahmed, H. (2002), corporate governance in Islamic financial institutions, occasional papers. No. 6 Islamic Research and Training Institute, Islamic Development Bank.

➢ Chapra, M.U. 1986. Towards a just monetary system (1st Ed.) Leicester: The Islamic Foundation.

➢ Chong, B.S. and Liu, M.H. (2008), Islamic banking: Interest Free or interest-based? Pacific-Basin Finance Journal, 17:125-144.

➢ Clark, L. A., & Watson, D. (1995). Constructing Validity: Basic Issues in Objective Scale Development. Psychological Assessment © 1995 by the American Psychological Association. Vol. 7, No. 3, 309-319.

➢ Cohen, L, Manion, L, Morrison, K & Morrison, RB, 2007, Research Methods in Education, Routledge.

➢ Cole HL, Kocherlakota N (1998). Zero Nominal Interest Rates: Why they're good and get them. Fed. Reserve Bank Minneapolis Q., 22: 2-10.

➢ Cooper, C. R., & Schindler, P. S. (2008). Business research methods (10 ed.). Boston: McGraw-Hill.

➢ Court, D., French, T. D., McGuire, T. I. & Partington, M. 1999. Marketing in 3-D. The Mckinsey Quarterly, 4, 6-17.

➢ Creswell, (1994) Research Design: Qualitative and Quantitative Approaches. Thousand Oaks; London: SAGE.

➢ D. Fatmawati, N.M. Ariffin, N.Z. Abidin, et al., (2020), Shari'ah governance in Islamic banks: Practices, practitioners and praxis, Global Finance Journal.

➢ Daher, H., Masih, M., and Ibrahim, M. (2015), The unique risk exposures of Islamic banks' capital buffers: a dynamic panel data analysis. Journal of International Financial Markets, Institutions & Money 36(2015), 36e52.

➢ Daniel WW (1999). Biostatistics: A Foundation for Analysis in the Health Sciences. 7th edition. New York: John Wiley & Sons.

➢ DeLeeuw, E., Hox, J. & Dillman, D. (2008) International Handbook of Survey Methodology. New York: Lawrence Erlbaum Associates.

➢ Draft Report of the Working Group to review the Banking Regulation Act, 1949, Indian Banks' Association , May 2008.

➢ Dusuki, W.A. and Abdullah, I.N. (2007), Why do Malaysian customers patronize Islamic banks? International Journal of Bank Marketing, 25(3):142-160.

➢ EI-Ashker, A. (1987). The Islamic Business Enterprises. Kent, Croom Helm.

➢ EI-Gamal, M. (2000). An Economic Explication of the Prohibition of Riba in Classical Islamic Jurisprudence. The Third Harvard University Forum on Islamic Finance, Cambridge, Center for Middle Eastern Studies, Harvard University.

➢ El Hamiani Khatat, M., (2016), Monetary policy in the presence of Islamic banking. IMF Working Paper No. WP/16/72. (March2016).

➢ Elghuweel, M. I., Ntim, C., Opong, K., and Avison, L. (2017), Corporate Governance, Islamic Governance and Earnings Management in Oman: A new Empirical Insights from A Behavioral Theoretical Framework, Journal of Accounting in Emerging Economies, 7(2).

➢ Ergec, E. and Arslan, B., (2013), Impact of interest rates on Islamic and conventional banks: The Case of Turkey. Applied Economics 45 (17), 2381–2388.

➢ Eriksson, K. (2008), The future of retail banking. International Journal of Bank Marketing, 26(1). Guest Editor.

➢ Errico, L. and M. Farahbakash (1998). "Islamic Banking: Issues in Prudential Regulation and Supervision." IMF.

➢ Field, A.(2009). Discovering statistics using SPSS (3rd Ed.). Beverly Hills, CA: Sage Publications.

➢ Fisher, R. J., Maltz, E. & Jaworski, B. J. (1997) Enhancing communication between marketing and engineering: the moderating role of relative functional identification Journal of Marketing 61(3) pp.54-70.

➢ Friedman M (1969). The optimum quantity of money, The Optimum Quantity of Money and Other Essays. Chicago: Aldine, pp. 1-50.

➤ Funfgeld, B. and Wang, M. (2009), Attitudes and behavior in everyday finance: evidence from Switzerland. International Journal of Bank Marketing, 27(2):108-128.

➤ Gambling, T. and R. Karim (1991). Business and Accounting Ethics in Islam. London, Mansell Publishing Limited.

➤ Gerrard, J.B. and Cunningham. P. (1997), Islamic banking: a study in Singapore. International Journal of Bank Marketing, 15:204-216.

➤ Ghannadian, F.F. and Goswami, G, (2004), Developing economy banking: the case of Islamic banks, International Journal of Social Economics, 31(8):740-752.

➤ Ghayad, R. (2008), Corporate Governance and the Global Performance of Islamic Banks. Humanomics, 24(3), 207–216.

➤ Ginena, K., and Hamid, A., (2015), Foundations of Shariah Governance of Islamic Banks. Wiley.

➤ Gowhar Bashir Ahangar & Ashaq Hussain Ganie (2013), Scope of Islamic Banking in India, 2(5), 266-269.

➤ Grassa, R. (2016), Corporate Governance and Credit Rating in Islamic Banks: Does Shariah Governance Matters? Journal of Management and Governance, 20(4).

➤ Grassa, R., (2013), Shariah Supervisory System in Islamic Financial Institutions: New Issues and Challenges: A Comparative Analysis between Southeast Asia Models and GCC Models. Humanomics, 29(4), 333–348.

➤ Grassa, R., (2015), Shariah Supervisory System in Islamic Financial Institutions across the OIC Member Countries: An Investigation of Regulatory Frameworks. Journal of Financial Regulation and Compliance, 23(2), 135–160.

➤ Grassa, R., & Matoussi, H., (2014a), Corporate Governance of Islamic Banks in GCC and SE Asia. International Journal of Islamic and Middle Eastern Finance and Management, 7(3), 346–362.

➤ Grassa, R., and Matoussi, H., (2014b), Is Corporate Governance Different for Islamic banks? A Comparative Analysis between the Gulf Cooperation Council and Southeast Asian countries. International Journal of Business Governance and Ethics, 9(1), 27–51.

➤ Griffin, A. & Hauser, J. R. (1996) Integrating R&D and marketing: a review and analysis of the literature Journal of Product Innovation 13(3) pp.191-216.

➤ Gunputh, R. P. (2014), Micro-credit in conventional banking: Would Islamic banking be the golden age for entrepreneurs? The Mauritius case, study. Journal of Social and Development Sciences, 5(1), 14–25.

- Gupta N, (2017), **IFB** in India, International Journal of Advance Research, Ideas and Innovations in Technology, Volume3, Issue1, ISSN: 2454-132X.

- Hair, J. F. Jr., Babin, B., Money, A. H., & Samouel, P. (2003). Essential of business research methods. John Wiley & Sons: United States of America.

- Hair, J. F., Anderson, R. E., Tatham, R. L., & Black, W. C. (1998). Multivariate Data Analysis (Fifth ed.). Upper Saddle River, New Jersey: Prentice-Hall, Inc.

- Hamza, H., (2016), Does investment deposit return in Islamic banks reflect PLS principle? Borsa Istanbul Review 16-1, 32e42.

- Hamza, H., Saadaoui, Z., (2013), Investment deposits, risk-taking and capital decisions in Islamic banks. Studies in Economics and Finance 30 (3), 244–265 Emerald Group.

- Har, K.Y. and Ta, H.P. (2000), A study of bank selection decisions in Singapore using the analytical hierarchy process, International Journal of Bank Marketing, 18(4):170-178.

- Haron, S. (1996), Competition and other external determinants of the profitability of Islamic banks. Islamic Economic Studies, 4(1), 49–64.

- Hasan, Z., (2011), A Survey on Shari'ah Governance Practices in Malaysia, GCC Countries and the UK: Critical Appraisal. International Journal of Islamic and Middle Eastern Finance and Management, 4(1), 30–51.

- Hasan, Z., (2012), Shari'ah Governance in Islamic banks. Edinburgh University Press.

- Hasan, Z., (2014), In search of the perceptions of the Shari'ah scholars on Shari'ah governance system, International Journal of Islamic and Middle Eastern Finance and Management, 7(1), 22–36, https://doi.org/10.1108/IMEFM-07-2012-0059.

- Hassan, M. K., and Bashir, A. H. M. (2003), Determinants of Islamic banking profitability, vol. 7.

- Hussain, M., Shahmoradi, A., Turk, R. (2015), An overview of Islamic finance. International Monetary Fund Working Paper, WP/15/120.

- Ibrahim, B.F.M. and Seoweng, O., (2006), Shariah compliance in real estate investment.

- IFSB Islamic Financial Services Board, (2009), Guiding Principles on Shari'ah Governance Systems for Institutions Offering Islamic Financial Services, Islamic Financial Service Board, Kuala Lumpur. Retrieved from www.ifsb.org.

- Iqbal, Z., and Mirakhor, A. (2004), A stakeholders model of corporate governance of firm in Islamic Economic System. Islamic Economic Studies, 11(2), 43e64. IRTI.

- Jammeh Basainey Ebrahima (2010), Prospects and Challenges of Islamic Banking in USA, Journal of Social Science Research Network.

- Johnson, R.A., & Wichern, D.W. (1982). Applied multivariate statistical analysis. Englewood Cliffs, NJ: Prentice-Hall.

- Kader, R.A., Leong, Y.K., (2009), The impact of interest rate changes on Islamic bank financing. International Review of Business Research Papers 5 (3), 189–201.

- Kahf, M. and Hamadi, C., (2014), An attempt to develop Shariah compliant Liquidity management instruments for the financier of last resort: With Reference to Qatar Development Plan. Islamic Economic Studies 22 (May (1)), 109–138.

- Khadar A. & Aneesh. A (2019), Islamic banking in India: Concept, Principles and Developments, Conference: A two day International Conference on "Contemporary innovations in Industry and Commerce, At: Mangalore University.

- Khan, M. A. (1994). Accounting Issues and concepts for Islamic Banking. Accounting Issues in Islamic Banking. London, Institute of Islamic Banking and Insurance: pp.1-45.

- Khan, T. and Ahmed, H. (2001), Risk Management: An Analysis of Issues in Islamic Financial Industry. Occasional Paper 5, Islamic Development Bank.

- Kolsi, M. C., and Grassa, R. (2017), Did Corporate Governance Mechanisms Affect Earnings Management? Further Evidence from GCC Islamic Banks. International Journal of Islamic and Middle Eastern Finance and Management, 10(1).

- Kusuma, H., and Ayumardani, A., (2016), The Corporate Governance Efficiency and Islamic Bank Performance: An Indonesian Evidence. Polish Journal of Management Studies, 13(1), 111–120.

- Lewis, M. and L. Algaoud (2001). Islamic Banking. Cheltenham, E. Elgar.

- Maali, B. (2005). Financial accounting and reporting in Islamic banks: the case of Jordan. School of Management. Southampton, University of Southampton. Ph.D.

- Mashhour, N. (1996). Social and Solidarity Activity in Islamic Banks. Cairo, the International Institute of Islamic Thought. [Arabic].

- Matthews, R. Tlemsani and Siddique A (2004) Islamic banking and the mortgage market in the UK, in Shanmugam, Balaet.al (2004). Islamic banking: an international perspective, Serdang, Malaysia: university Putra Malaysia press.

- McCawley, T. (2004), Islam's edicts, Far Eastern Economic Review, 167(5):36.

164

➢ McKinsey and Company, Islamic Finance Interest Group, (2005), Islamic banking competitiveness report, tracking an industry in transition. In: 12th World Islamic Banking Conference, Manama, Bahrain.

➢ Mehtab, H., Zaheer, Z., and Ali, S. (2015), Knowledge, attitudes and practices (KAP) survey: A case study on Islamic banking at Peshawar, Pakistan. FWU Journal of Social Sciences, 9(2), 1.

➢ Mersni, H., and Ben Othman, H. (2016), The Impact of Corporate Governance Mechanisms on Earnings Management in Islamic Banks in the Middle East Region. Journal of Islamic Accounting and Business Research, 7(4), 318–348.

➢ Mollah, S., and Karim, W. (2011), Does Corporate Governance Model of Interest-Free Banks Provide Better Protection against Financial Crisis? Empirical Investigation on Corporate Governance perspectives of the interest-free banks globally, In 8th International Conference on Islamic Economics and Finance.

➢ Mollah, S., and Zaman, M., (2015), Shari'ah Supervision, Corporate Governance and Performance: Conventional vs. Islamic Banks. Journal of Banking & Finance, 58, 418–435.

➢ Mollah, S., Hassan, M. K., Al Farooque, O., and Mobarek, A., (2017), The Governance, Risk-taking, and Performance of Islamic Banks. Journal of Financial Services Research, (51), 195–219.

➢ Mondher Bellalah, (2013). Islamic Banking and Finance, Cambridge Scholars Publishing, UK, pp. 58-59.

➢ Moore, E. J. (2009), The International Handbook of Islamic Banking and Finance. Kent Global Professional Publishing.

➢ Naser, A.L. and A-L Khatib, K. (1999), Islamic banking: A study of customer satisfaction and preferences in Jordan. International Journal of Bank Marketing, 17:135-150.

➢ Nienhaus, V. (1983), Profitability of Islamic PLS banks competing with interest banks: Problems and prospects. Journal of Research in Islamic Economics, 1(1), 37–47.

➢ O'Leary Z. 2004 "The essential guide to doing research". Sage.

➢ Omar, M.A. (1999). "Islamic rules for the preparation of accounting standards." Al iqtisadi Al islami (220): 30-35.

➢ Pallant, J. (2007). SPSS survival guide: A step by step guide to data analysis using SPSS for windows (version 10), NSW: Allen & Unwin.

➢ Patel, E. (2006), Fundamentals of Islamic finance. Accountancy SA, 18–19.

➢ Presley, J. R. (1988). Directory of Islamic financial institutions. London, Croom Helm.

➢ Rahman, A. A., Latif, R. A., Mud, R., and Abdullah, M. A. (2014), Failure and potential of profit-loss sharing contracts: a perspective of new institutional, economic (NIE) theory. Pacific-Basin Finance Journal, 136e151.

➢ Raqeeb, H.A (2012). India needs Islamic banking for inclusion growth and infrastructure development. Mainstream (19).

➢ Remenyi D Williams, B Money A Swartz E, 1998, Doing Research in Business, Sage, London.

➢ Rosly, S.A., (1999), Al-bay Bithaman Ajil Financing: Impacts on Islamic banking performance. Thunderbird International Business Review 41, 461–480.

➢ Saadallah, R. (1994). "Concept of Time in Islamic Economics". Islamic Economic Studies 2(1): pp.81-102.

➢ Safiullah, M., and Shamsuddin, A., (2018), Risk in Islamic banking and corporate governance. Pacific-Basin Finance Journal, 47, 129–149.

➢ Saidi, A.T. (2007), Relationships between ethical and Islamic banking systems and its business management implications. South Africa Journal of Business Management, 1:43-49.

➢ Saif-Alyousfi, A. Y., Saha, A., and Md-Rus, R. (2017), Shareholders' value of Saudi commercial banks: A comparative evaluation between Islamic and conventional banks using CAMEL parameters. International Journal of Economics and Financial Issues, 7(1), 97–105.

➢ Saunders, G.S., Bendixen, M. and Abratt, R. (2007), Banking patronage motives of the urban informal pool. Journal of Services Marketing, 21(1):52-63.

➢ Schoon N, (2016) Modern Islamic banking: products and processes in practice. Shahid, M. S., Hassan, M. and Rizwan, M. (2015), Determinants of Islamic banks' profitability: Some evidence from Pakistan. Pakistan Journal of Islamic Research.

➢ Sharma. A, Shukla. S. K. Samir, (2015), Islamic Banking: An Opportunity for India, Intl. J. Adv. Res. Comm & Mgmt, 1(1):22-27.

➢ Singh, K. (2007) "Quantitative Social Research Methods" SAGE Publications, p.64.

➢ Srivatsa, H.S. and Srinivasan, R. (2008), New age youth banking behavior: an explorative study in the Indian banking sector, Journal of Services Research, 8(2):53-71.

➤ Sukmana, R. and Kassim, S.H., (2010), Roles of the Islamic Banks in the Monetary Transmission Process in Malaysia. International Journal of Islamic and Middle Eastern Finance and Management 3 (1), 7–19.

➤ Swaraj. A (2019), Exploratory Research: Purpose And Process, Parisheelan Vol.-XV, No.- 2, ISSN 0974 7222.

➤ Tabachnick, B.G., & Fidell, L.S. (2007). Using multivariate statistics (5th Ed.). Boston, MA: Allyn and Bacon.

➤ Taylor, T. and J. Evans (1987). "Islamic Banking and the Prohibition of Usury in Western Economic Thought." National Westminster Bank Quarterly Review November: pp.15-27.

➤ Usmani, T. (2002). An introduction to Islamic finance. The Hague; London, Kluwer Law International.

➤ Walliman, N. S. & Walliman N. (2011) "Research methods: the basics" Taylor and Francis.

➤ Weill, L., (2011), Do Islamic banks have greater market power? Comparative Economic Studies 53, 291–306.

➤ Wilson, R. (1997). Islamic Finance. London, FT Financial Publishing Pearson Professional Limited.

➤ Wisker, G. (2008), The Postgraduate Research Handbook. 2nd Ed. New York: Palgrave.

➤ Wulandari S Y, Laelasari R and Rakhman F., (2020). Analysis of Strengths, Weaknesses, Opportunities, Threats on Multi Jasa Financing at PT BPRS Daarut Tauhid. Advances in Social Science, Education and Humanities Research, volume 536 Proceedings of the First International Conference on Science, Technology, Engineering and Industrial Revolution (ICSTEIR 2020).

➤ Zahediasl. S & Ghasemi, A. (2012), Normality Tests for Statistical Analysis: A Guide for Non-Statisticians, International Journal of Endocrinology and Metabolism 10(2):486-489 DOI:10.5812/ijem.3505.

➤ Zaher, T., Hassan, K., (2001), A comparative literature survey of Islamic finance and banking. Finance Mark. Inst. Instrum. 10 (4), 155–199.

➤ Zainol, Z., and Kassim, S. H. (2010), An analysis of Islamic banks' exposure to rate of return risk. Journal of Economic Cooperation and Development, 31(1), 59e84.

➤ Zikmund, William. G (2003). Business Research Method, 7th Ed, South- Western, A division of Thomson Learning.

Milton Keynes UK
Ingram Content Group UK Ltd.
UKHW032228120324
439302UK00013B/744